E
Wild Food
Guide

Easy
Wild Food
Guide

Written, painted and photographed by Neil Fletcher

Additional text, paintings and photographs by
Gill Tomblin, Keith Rushforth and David Pegler

AURUM PRESS

First published 2007 by Aurum Press Ltd
7 Greenland Street, London, NW1 0ND
www.aurumpress.co.uk

A catalogue record of this book is available from the British Library

ISBN-10 1 84513 254 8
ISBN-13   978 1 84513 254 5

Printed in Portugal by Printer Portuguesa

Origination by Universal Graphics, Singapore

Conceived, edited, designed and produced by Duncan Petersen Publishing
C7 Old Imperial Laundry, Warriner Gardens, London, SW11 4XW.

Editor Hermione Edwards
Production Editor Jacqui Sayers
Designer Ian Midson
Editorial Director Andrew Duncan

Photography credits: see page 253

Foreword

Without farmers growing crops and herding livestock, without butchers, bakers, distribution networks and shopkeepers - without, in short, a commercial food industry - who knows how slow the pace of human development would have been? Getting food to the table is both energy and time consuming, leaving little for man's more rarified, but equally important, endeavours, such as inventing computers and writing books.

We are, however, shamefully reliant on ready-to-serve food. We have become all too used to the supermarket; we even order our food through the Internet without leaving the house. When it arrives, it is packaged in plastic, processed out of recognition, pumped full of chemicals, and all too often lacking in flavour. We have lost touch with the reality of where our food originates from, what it used to taste, smell and feel like; what it is.

Intensive food production has resulted in a major loss of wildlife worldwide, and this applies as much to the birds and insects of Europe as it does to the riches of the tropical rainforest, cut down to make hamburger beef. New viruses and other pathogens are blooming as a result of intensive animal rearing, modern crops have to be plied with chemicals to keep them alive, and now we are turning to genetic engineering in the hope of righting these wrongs.

There are some positive signs. Interest in organic produce has blossomed, no longer a quirky fad, but mainstream enough even for the supermarkets to devote large amounts of space to it. Recently, the sale of seeds for growing vegetables exceeded the sale of those for growing flowers for the first time in one Western European country. People want to get back, in part at least, to the reality of food unadulterated by modern processing. Nothing is more unadulterated than wild food.

That's not to say we should eat nothing else: if you did, in Western Europe, you would starve pretty quickly. But eating food from the wild does reconnect you with where food comes from. It may well give you a transitory, but valuable, sense of independence from the commercial food chain. It will save you a little money. And, perhaps more significant, it may teach you to be less wasteful with what you buy in the supermarket. What's more, it is great fun.

Neil Fletcher
Spring 2007

Lime leaves

Contents

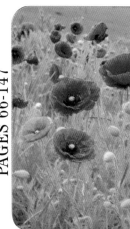

AUTUMN

WINTER

About this book

CAN A GUIDE TO WILD FOOD REALLY BE EASY?

Yes, provided that the key facts - those that point to the right name for the right plant, tree, fungus or sea food - are presented in an exceptionally clear, self-evident way. In this guide we make an unusually clear distinction between overall appearance (in the photo on the right hand page) and the fine details that pin down identification (in the artwork panel on the left hand page).

HOW EASY?

In making this the easy wild food guide, we have concentrated on several key points:

• **A manageable number of species, carefully selected.** We have deliberately left out wild food that was used in the past but no longer makes sense to collect - unless you happen to be starving. Every wild food in this guide is worth the effort of collecting. They are not all as good as each other, but each and every one is considered interesting and worthwhile by the author - who has tried them all. Read the main text, and you'll quickly discover their relative value and interest as a food.

• **Worry-free identification.** This guide carries more identification clues than any other wild food guide we've seen, presented in the most straightforward manner possible. This is invaluable because there's nothing worse than nagging doubts about what you might - or might not - be eating.

• **Simple language.** The text is free of jargon and technical terms, and explains simply the key features to look out for, as well as the general appearance.

• **Simple 'boilerplate' recipes** which are easy to follow, fun to improvise on, and don't ask for ingredients you are unlikely to have in the store cupboard. I think it's best to cook wild food well, but spontaneously, with the aim of bringing out its essential flavour. Many of the cooking suggestions in this book are designed with this in mind - they are not really recipes as such, and can be applied to many different wildfoods.

• **Imaginative ways of using wild food** you'd never have thought of. See duck breast and Fairy Ring Champignon salad, page 64, Wild Service Berry fruit cake, page 162, and Heather tea, page 106 - to list but three.

Fairy Ring Champignons

Collecting plants for food

Perhaps the best place to start is with wild plants and trees: they are generally easy to find and identify; some need minimal preparation - indeed many can be eaten raw.

Hop leaves and flowers

The first step is to correctly identify your quarry. Make sure that all of the identification characters featured in this book for the plant match your specimen - leaf shape and leaf arrangement, flowers, bracts and fruit - don't be satisfied until you are certain that what you have gathered is exactly the same as what you see on the page.

One of the joys of discovering the identity of a plant species is that you can go on getting to know it long after you have put a name to it. Be receptive and observant, and you'll begin to take in plant characteristics that can't be explained easily in words or pictures: an overall impression of its essential quality, size and shape (what birdwatchers call jizz), which enable you to recognize a plant even from a distance. You should also come to know which habitat a species prefers, and with which other species it grows in association.

It is especially important to correctly identify plants of the carrot family, whose flowers are held on stalks arranged like the spokes of a wheel (umbels) and often have fern-like leaves. This family contains many edible species (including carrot, of course, though the wild form is not worth gathering), but it also contains a few seriously poisonous species. In particular, Cow Parsley may be confused with the deadly Hemlock (Conium maculatum), which, incidentally, smells offensively of mouse urine; or the poisonous Fool's Parsley (Aethusa cynapium).

Choose your collecting ground with care. Many urban green spaces are the very places where people choose to exercise dogs. The same is true of paths close to car parks and lay-bys. Avoid plants that may have been peed on (or worse) by dogs: a shower of rain is not enough to remove dangerous pathogens. Dog latrines are often identified by patches of dark green, luxuriant growth.

Also, avoid collecting plants from places adjacent to farmland that may have been sprayed recently with pesticides. These chemicals are harmful when fresh; if in any doubt, avoid such locations. Beware, too, of road verges that may have sprayed, perhaps to eradicate pernicious weeds. Japanese Knotweed, for example, is regularly sprayed with herbicide by local authorities: there may be a noticeable 'chemical' smell in the vicinity, or plants may be turning yellow or looking sickly.

Always give leaves and fruit a rinse before adding them to a salad or cooking them. Flowers, however, such as those of Elder, should not be washed, as the delicious nectar, and therefore the flavour, will be rinsed away too. Instead, give them a thorough shake in order to persuade insects that it's time to leave. Flowers, of course, don't stay open for long, so they don't pick up much dirt.

Collecting mushrooms for food

There are two essential pieces of equipment for the fungi forager. The first is a small kitchen knife. This is useful for removing tough fungi that grow on trees, such as Oyster Mushrooms and Chicken-of-the-Woods. It can also be used to lift up the base of a soil-dwelling specimen to examine whether a bulb or volva is present - sometimes an important factor in identification. Moreover, it should be used to cut off any parts with soil clinging to them, since when soil dries it tends to fall into the gills, from which it is difficult to extract.

The second is a basket. I think that a basket is essential for collecting even a small quantity of fungi, since any kind of bag causes specimens to be squeezed together, damaging them. A flat, open basket, on the other hand, allows the mushrooms to get plenty of ventilation, and stops you stacking them too deeply. Place your trophies in the basket gills downwards, so that any dirt doesn't fall into the gills beneath.

WHEN TO LOOK

The main mushrooming season is rooted firmly in the autumn. This is when the soil is warm, and when there is usually enough rainfall to create the moist conditions necessary for fungal growth. Of course, such conditions may occur in the summer too, so the season may start early, or late - it all depends on the weather conditions. Weather aside, some years are better for some species, or groups of species, than others, for reasons that are difficult to determine. Some years are great for Parasols, Charcoal Burners and Horse Mushrooms, but very disappointing for the Penny Bun or Cep. Other years see the woods flooded with Penny Buns and other Boletes. This is part of the magic of mushroom hunting - there is no way of knowing quite what you will find on any particular outing. It is crucial, however, not to forget the spring season. This is all too often passed over by the mushroom enthusiast, who dreams of the months to come, but the St. George's Mushroom, and especially the Morel, are highly prized, and appear in April and May.

WHERE TO LOOK

In general, fungi prefer to grow in moist places on soils that are rich in humus. It is important to remember that the mushrooms we seek out are the fruiting bodies of the fungus, the organs they produce in order to disperse their spores. The main body of the fungus is the mycelium: thousands of microscopic threads, which work their way through the soil feeding on decaying matter. Most mushrooms are to be found in woodland, both because of the large amount of leaf litter and rotten wood, and also because some species grow in association with the roots of particular trees.

Some species, such as Parasols and Field Mushrooms, are more likely to be found in meadows and pastures. The common factor, however, is that fungi generally prefer habitats that have been left undisturbed for a long time, so ancient woodlands with plenty of old trees are often much better than relatively newly planted ones. Similarly, pastures that have been under the same system of management, without having been ploughed for decades, are far more likely to yield abundant crops of fungi. You will learn to recognise the best sites, perhaps at first because of the large numbers of fungi they produce, but later by other clues such as the plants that grow there.

PREPARING FUNGI

It really is worth 'processing' the results of your collecting foray as soon as you get home. Clean the mushrooms of any loose dirt or grit, or give them a wipe with a kitchen towel, but don't wash them, as they absorb water very readily and become mushy. It may also be worth making a few exploratory slices through them, for even apparently healthy specimens can sometimes harbor insect larvae, and should be discarded. Most mushrooms will keep in a refrigerator for 24 hours, and should either be preserved or eaten within that time. An exception is the Shaggy Ink Cap, which degrades quickly into a black, slimy mess, even if kept cool.

Correct identification of fungi is, of course, essential. Don't eat any fungi unless you are 100 per cent sure of its identification. Although this guide aims to give as much information as possible for correct identification, it is no substitute for experience gained in the field under the guidance of an expert. There are organized fungi forays in most areas during the autumn, often with edible species as the focus, and confidence can only come with handling, smelling, and seeing the variation in colour and shape that can occur even within the same species.

Even when a mushroom's identity has been confirmed, remember that different species affect people in different ways, and you should always only try a small piece of an unfamiliar species for the first time. Wait a few hours before eating more to ensure that there are no unpleasant consequences. Never eat a wild mushroom raw (with the exception of truffles): even the tiniest piece of some species, such as Honey Fungus, can cause severe gastric problems, though they are harmless when cooked.

In this guide, the Lookalikes box on the right hand page of each two-page mushroom spread is essential reading: it will tell you if any poisonous species can easily be confused with the edible fungus in question. Again, if any doubt, do not eat.

PRESERVING FUNGI

Fungi can be enjoyed all year round if preserved. This is a popular practice in Eastern Europe, not so common in the West. Different methods are suitable for different species, and some species do not preserve well at all.

Chanterelle

DRYING

Drying is a great way to keep mushrooms available for future use in soups and stews, but only works with varieties that reconstitute well, and this particularly applies to boletes such as the Penny Bun and Bay Bolete. Cut the mushrooms up into thin slices, then lay them out on to a tea towel over a tray, or a square of wire mesh. A wire rack may seem suitable at first, but the slices shrink considerably as they dry and may fall between the wires. The tray then needs to be placed where there is constant warm, dry air: over a central heating radiator, for example, or in an oven set to its coolest setting and with the door left open. It can take a day or two for the pieces to dry fully over a radiator. They should be brittle, and will snap, rather than bend, when they are dry enough.

Morels, Chanterelles and Horn of Plenty can all be dried by threading them on a piece of string using a heavy needle, then hanging in a warm place. Keep the dried mushrooms in sealed jars until required. They will need to be reconstituted in very hot water for half an hour or so before being used in a recipe. Be sure to use the liquor that is left over from this, as it will be full of the flavour of the mushrooms.

Brown Birch Boletes

FREEZING

Boletes can be frozen whole, provided they are dry, though it may be more convenient to slice them first. Parasols, Shaggy Ink Caps and Saffron Milk Caps should be blanched first by immersing them in boiling water, a little at a time, for one minute. This rids them of any toxins and helps to preserve their texture when thawed again. Be sure that they are completely cool and dry before putting them in the freezer. Chanterelles, Chicken-of-the-Woods and Honey Fungus should be sautéed first in butter and oil before freezing, again to remove toxins and to enhance their flavour.

A mixture of fungi can be preserved for use in soups and stews by sautéing them first, then using a blender to chop them into a coarse paste. This can be spooned into the compartments of an ice cube tray and frozen. One or two cubes will be enough to add plenty of mushroom flavour to any dish.

PRESERVING IN OIL

Most species can be preserved in oil. Young specimens are best: they should be cleaned and sliced, then boiled in a mixture of 300 ml of water with 200 ml of white wine vinegar for 10 minutes. Put the mushrooms into a sealable jar with your favourite spices such as bay leaves, peppercorns, cinnamon, cloves and garlic, then top up with best quality olive oil so the mushrooms are completely covered. Seal the jar and keep in a cool, dark cupboard for six months or so.

Mushroom safety

1 Be aware that there are many more poisonous mushrooms than edible ones.

2 Find out how to recognize poisonous mushrooms by buying a guide that illustrates them in detail. One of the best available is The Easy Edible Mushroom Guide. Also, learn the poisonous species from an expert, but make sure he/she really is an expert. Be aware that there is no 100 per cent foolproof rule to say whether a species is poisonous, so unless you are sure that a mushroom is edible, don't eat it.

3 Some individuals are intolerant of certain mushrooms, finding them hard to digest and suffering from stomach upset. This is not the same as real mushroom poisoning.

4 If trying a wild mushroom for the first time, even if you have identified it positively, only eat a small amount. Keep at least one fruit body uneaten, in case it is needed for identification.

5 Learn the symptoms of true mushroom poisoning, again from an expert and from a field guide.

6 If you suspect true mushroom poisoning after eating fungi:
- get immediate medical help. If symptoms occur six to ten hours or more after eating, go straight to hospital.
- induce vomiting by tickling the back of the throat. Using a strong saline solution is not recommended. A bland drink, such as milk or water, may then be given to dilute remaining toxins.
- retain evidence of the fungus consumed, including any regurgitated material, so a professional mycologist has a chance of identifying the offender.

Shaggy Ink Cap

Collecting seafood

Seafood, collected from the shoreline, is a ready source of protein, and in the past has kept alive entire populations of coastal-dwelling peoples. Some seafoods have changed wildly in value according to the fashions of the day.

Cockle

Seafood can, of course, cause stomach upset. In some cases, this may be due to an individual's intolerance. Very commonly, however, it is because the item has been dead too long, or because the animal has absorbed toxins. For this reason, reputable restaurants insist that shellfish such as crabs, lobsters and mussels are delivered alive, so they can be absolutely certain that the animal has not been dead for a long period. These creatures decompose rapidly, and quickly become dangerous. Crustaceans such as prawns cannot be transported alive, so they are cooked immediately, then deep-frozen, and sadly this denies the consumer their fresh flavour.

Molluscs such as mussels, cockles, razor shells and oysters are filter feeders. They pass gallons of sea water through their bodies, filtering out plankton primarily, but also sewage particles and associated bacteria. These are more prevalent in the summer when the sea is warm (thus promoting the growth of harmful bacteria), and when there is less rainfall to flush sewage away from the coast, and fewer storms to keep the inshore waters fresh. So these shellfish should be collected in the winter, when the risk of harmful substances in the flesh is much lower. Mussels and oysters bought from fishmongers have usually been farmed in areas of clean sea that are carefully monitored for levels of pathogens.

It is important to collect seafood well away from places where there are sewage outfalls or other sources of pollution, such as coastal towns, villages and harbours. In other words, if a stretch of coast is easily accessible, it's not ideal for collecting seafood. A trip to a wild, lonely, rocky coast is more rewarding, and more likely to produce safe seafood.

Such restrictions do not apply to crabs, prawns and shrimps, which feed directly on vegetation or other matter. They also happen to be more prevalent and flavoursome in the summer.

As with plants, you will, after a little practice, learn to recognise the 'look' of the most fruitful areas for seafood: the kind of rock pool that may shelter a crab, the types of seaweed bed that will produce the most winkles. It is really worthwhile to visit the coast at low tide to explore exposed rock pools. For this purpose, tide tables are invaluable - available from fishing shops, local newspapers and the Internet. It is best of all to visit during the lowest ('spring') tides, which coincide every fortnight or so with the full or new moon. Then you have the best chance of finding a large crab.

Common Prawn

Finally, take great care not to get cut off by the returning tide. It is all too easy to become engrossed in the possibilities of a promising rock pool, to find yourself trapped in a cove with no way of escape. Equally, when out on the sand flats searching for cockles, the tide may cut off your return, even though there is a clear view back to safety. In minutes, incoming water can turn previously firm ground into impassable mud or quicksand.

Humane treatment of shellfish and snails

One of the many pleasures of collecting wild food is that you can be sure of how it has been treated. This is especially relevant with seafood. Since one should never eat any kind of seafood that is already dead when found, it follows that you also have to face the task of dispatching it.

The usual method is fast immersion in boiling water. Some say that crabs and lobsters should be placed in cold water, which is slowly heated to boiling point, and that they 'fall asleep' during the process. This method, however, is not recommended by animal welfare organizations. The immediate insertion into boiling water is generally agreed to be the best for small animals - snails, prawns, shrimps, mussels, cockles, razor shells, winkles and whelks. Because of their size, their body tissues are heated to high temperature almost immediately, and death is more or less instant.

We can never know exactly what molluscs and crustaceans feel. They clearly respond to many stimuli, but do not have brains and nervous systems constructed along the same lines as those of humans. So larger molluscs and crustaceans pose a problem. Live crabs thrown into boiling water show signs of distress, indeed they often shed legs and claws. This is unacceptable for fishmongers, ethics apart, since the crabs need to be sold in one piece.

There are two acceptable ways of killing crabs. The first requires a degree of skill, and involves spiking the two main nerve centres. A large, blunt screwdriver is the best tool. Poke it into the mouth of the crab and push it up between the eyes to destroy the nerve centre there. Then turn the crab over on to its back, lift up the pointed tail flap, and locate the small hole in the shell underneath. Insert the screwdriver sharply into this and move the tip of the blade backwards to destroy the second nerve centre. It is worth asking your fishmonger for more detailed advice before attempting this, as it needs to performed with confidence to be successful.

A less gruesome technique, and the one recommended by animal welfare organizations, is to place the crab (or crayfish) in a plastic bag (to prevent it walking) and into the freezer, for two hours at -20°C. Unfortunately, most domestic freezers are set at -18°C, but -20°C should be possible through 'fast-freeze' option if there is one, or altering the thermostat control. The animal is not necessarily dead after this treatment, though it will not be moving. It should then be placed directly into rapidly boiling water, and cooked for the required length of time once the water is back to the boil. Handling and cooking these animals yourself means they get far more care and respect than could ever be achieved by a commercial enterprise, which makes its money by getting them to the supermarket shelf.

Garden Snail

Wild plants ideal for salads

Supermarkets sell bags of washed salad leaves at huge profit, yet year round common plants that are eminently suitable for the salad bowl surround us. The secret of a really good salad is something sharp, something bitter, and something a little bland to provide bulk and texture. Dressing, of course, is essential, and can be used to provide the sharpness. Use roughly five parts oil to one part acid. The oil could be a mixture of clean, flavourless oils such as groundnut or sunflower oil, and good olive oil; or introduce a flavourful oil such as walnut, hazelnut or sesame. The acid element can be wine, cider vinegar, balsamic vinegar, lemon juice, or yoghurt. Further flavour can be added to the dressing in the form of herbs, salt and pepper, crushed garlic, brown sugar, honey or mustard.

It's worth remembering that many of the following salad leaves such as Dandelion, Sorrel and Chickweed are available almost throughout the year:

Bulky leaves to act as the base:
Hawthorn leaves
Chickweed
Cornsalad
Dandelion
Ground Elder
Watercress (quite peppery)

Sharp-tasting leaves:
Wood Sorrel
Common Sorrel

To add a little bitterness:
Cow Parsley
Hairy Bittercress
Salad Burnet

...and for extra flavour:
Ramsons (garlic flavour)
Sweet Cicely leaves (anise flavour)
Wild Marjoram
Walnut
Hazel nuts
Beech nuts

Dandelion

Wild vegetables

Wild vegetables, in my view, are best served as a side dish in their own right, simply with a little butter and black pepper, in order simply to appreciate the flavour. They fall into two main categories: those that are cooked like asparagus and those that are cooked like spinach.

For the asparagus types, just a little light boiling is needed; or chargrill them, on a wire rack over hot coals if available, or on a hot skillet - preferably the sort with ridges. All the flavour is retained in the vegetables and none can dissolve into water.

Butter and pepper are good, but a Hollandaise sauce is a treat. (You can serve it in a separate bowl.) Clarify a pack (250 g) of butter by heating it gently in a pan until the solids fall to the bottom, then pour off the clear butter into a separate container and discard any remaining solids. Next prepare a bain-marie by placing a bowl (preferably stainless steel) over a pan half-filled with boiling water. Put 2 egg yolks in the bowl with 2 tbsp of water, and whisk until bulked up and creamy. Remove the bowl from the heat and whisk in the clarified butter a little at a time. Finally, add the juice of a lemon and a pinch of salt and white pepper.

The spinach types need minimal cooking: just sweat them in the water that clings to the leaves after washing. Even plants with coarse hairs such as Borage, Comfrey and Stinging Nettle will be soft and palatable after two or three minutes in a hot, covered pan. They can also be incorporated into soups, quiches, or stuffings for pasta.

Always choose the youngest shoots and leaves, as these will be the most tender, the least likely to be bitter, and the least damaged by insects. This also means that you can avoid destroying the whole plant.

Asparagus types:
Hop shoots
Good King Henry shoots
Marsh Samphire
Rock Samphire
Sea Kale shoots
Wild Asparagus
Alexanders shoots and flowerheads

Spinach types:
White dead-nettle leaves
Stinging nettle leaves
Sea beet leaves
Comfrey leaves
Borage leaves
Common Mallow leaves
Fat hen leaves

Fat Hen

Herbs and spices

Several of our wild foods do not in themselves provide a substantial meal, but are perfect for providing extra flavour to other dishes. Many of them can be dried or preserved for future use.

Cow Parsley	use like chervil in salads, soups and stews
Ramsons	has a wonderful aromatic garlic flavour
Horseradish	use for horseradish cream
Coriander	the leaves and seeds provide two different flavours
Common Poppy	sprinkle the seeds on vegetables, cakes and pastries
Sweet Cicely	gives a cool aniseed flavour with plenty of sweetness
Water Mint	is a sweeter version of Garden Mint
Wild Marjoram	is actually the culinary Oregano, perfect for Italian food
Wild Thyme	has a more subtle flavour than culinary Thyme
Juniper	the original gin flavouring that is perfect for dark meat
Fennel	gives a light aniseed flavour for fish and meat
Truffle	the world's most expensive food

Fennel

Sweets, jams, jellies and drinks

The following wild foods can all be used in one way or another to make desserts, cakes or tarts:

Sweet Violet flowers	**Fruits for jams and jellies:**	**…and for drinks:**
Primrose flowers	Bilberry	Lime Tree flowers
Raspberries	Cranberry	Elderflowers
Gooseberries	Cowberry	Meadowsweet flowers
Rosehip syrup	Gooseberry	Salad Burnet leaves
Wild Strawberries	Wild Service berries	Chicory root
Wild Service berries	Rowan	Dandelion root
Wild Cherries	Wild Plum	Heather flowers
Wild Plums	Crab Apple	Cranberries
Bilberries	Elderberry	Cowberries
Elderberries	Blackberry	Water Mint leaves
Blackberries	Dewberry	Balm leaves
Dewberries	Cloudberry	Juniper berries
Cloudberries		Sloe berries
Hazelnuts		Rosehip syrup
Beechnuts		
Walnuts		

Making jam - a basic recipe

Throughout this guide, I recommend wild foods as suitable for making jam or jelly. Doing so is easier and quicker than you might think, and is the perfect way to take advantage of the glut of berries and other fruits produced in summer and autumn. No special equipment is needed, other than a steel saucepan with a thick-bottomed base.

There are three basic requirements in jam making. First, sugar is needed not just to sweeten the taste, but also to act as a preservative. It prevents the fruit from becoming mouldy, so plenty is needed if the jam is to keep for any length of time. The second is pectin: the protein naturally present in fruit that makes it set. In wild foods pectin occurs in varying amounts, and, if a fruit is low in pectin, more needs to be added - usually in the form of a little lemon juice, or a special jam-making sugar that contains pectin. Added pectin is not, in fact, necessary for most of the wild fruits featured in this guide, except for Wild Strawberries - for which you would need more fruit than you are likely to find in the wild.

The third is total cleanliness. The fruit must be spotless; and the jars and lids should be boiled for five minutes and then put in a low oven to dry. Ideally, little wax paper discs, available from cook shops, should also be placed over the warm jam in the jar before closing it to seal out the air.

Always choose ripe fruit for making jam. Wash it, and cut away bruised or damaged parts. Put the fruit into the pan and gently simmer until it becomes a soft pulp: help the process with a wooden spoon. Then add the sugar, usually an equal weight to that of fruit. Lemon juice should also be added at this stage if necessary, 1 to 2 tbsp for each 500 g of fruit. The sugar needs to dissolve completely, but slowly, without being boiled. Ideally, use special preserving sugar in large lumps - it dissolves slowly. When the sugar is completely dissolved, the mixture should be brought up to boiling point and boiled rapidly until the setting point is reached. (This is the exciting part.) The setting point is reached at any point between 3 and 15 minutes. Stop the cooking as soon as it has been reached, or the jam will set solid, like tar.

Test for the setting point by placing a drop of the hot mixture on to a cold plate, placed in the refrigerator beforehand. Allow it to cool for about 30 seconds (remove the boiling jam from the heat while you're doing this), and then gently push your finger against the drop. If the surface of the drop wrinkles slightly, then its reached setting point. If it doesn't wrinkle and remains liquid, carry on cooking and try again a few minutes later. When ready, spoon the hot jam into the sterilized jars and seal them. Remember to label them with their contents and the date.

Raspberry

Making jelly - a basic recipe

Jellies differ from jams in that they are made from the juice of the fruit, without any of the fruit pulp itself, and are therefore clear in appearance. Jellies make a perfect accompaniment to game dishes, and are made even more interesting with the addition of a few chopped wild herbs.

The principals of jelly making are the same as described above for jam making, except that the simmered fruit pulp needs to be filtered to produce a clear fruit juice before any sugar is added. To do this, you will need a muslin bag. Put the simmered fruit pulp into the bag, and suspend it above the pan so that the juice can drain in. (Rig up a support for the muslin bag by turning a stool upside down, its feet in the air. Tie the four corners of the muslin to the feet of the stool.) You may think it worth buying a jelly bag from a cook shop: these come with their own little tripod for suspending the bag over a pan or jug.

Don't force the juice through the bag, tempting though this may be. It will encourage suspended particles to find their way through the muslin, which in turn makes the jelly cloudy. Often, pulp has to be left to drain in the bag overnight.

Once you have the juice, measure it, and allow 450 g of sugar for each 600 ml of juice. Less sugar can be used if desired, but the keeping quality of the jelly will be adversely affected: you run the risk of having to keep it in the refrigerator or even freeze it. Lemon juice should now also be added, 2 tbsp for each 600 ml of fruit juice. No lemon juice is needed for crab apple jelly, or if cooking apples are being used to bulk up the fruit, since they contain sufficient pectin. Apples make an excellent base for a jelly, to which can be added any other fruit which may be in shorter supply.

As with jam making, slowly dissolve the sugar, and only when it is all completely dissolved should you start to boil the mixture until setting point is reached (see the jam recipe). Pour the jelly into hot jars as quickly as possible, as it often sets very quickly - in fact it can begin to set in the pan before the last jar is filled.

Crab Apple

Cooking with wild food

Often enough, food collected from the wild can be treated in exactly the same way as you would its counterpart bought from a shop. But it's more fun to give wild food special treatment - after all, you've taken more trouble to collect it.

When trying out a wild food for the first time, I suggest that you cook it as simply as possible in order to discover its true flavour, untainted by other ingredients. Many of the cooking suggestions in this book are designed with just that in mind - they are not really recipes as such. It therefore follows that many of the suggestions given in this guide are interchangeable for different foods. Sauces made from wine reductions, butter or cream crop up regularly, and this defines my own style of cooking, but equally one could cook the foods in, for example, an oriental style - stir-fried in a wok and seasoned with soy sauce or nam pla fish sauce and lime juice. Before you opt for a cooking method, get to know the textures and flavours of a wild food, and choose the cooking method that seems most appropriate.

Some wild flavours are stronger than you may be used to. Supermarket salad leaves and vegetables, in particular, have had much of their flavour bred out of them in favour of high yield, attractive colour, pest resistance and consistency of size or shape. These attributes are designed solely for profit. The qualities we really prize in food are its taste, smell and texture, and wild food offers these naturally. So, if a new wild food seems at first a little strong, give it a second chance -you may grow to like it.

Wild food should not necessarily be a replacement for conventional foods. It should be part of a whole experience including the fun of collecting it and learning more about nature as you go. Cooking wild food outside, at the point of capture, in the company of friends is a delight. All you need is a few basic utensils, some clean water and a camping stove, or a beach fire.

If you're ambitious, you could, with a little preparation, hold a wild food dinner party. Start with, say, a few spiced beech or hazel nuts and a tipple of cranberry gin. Follow this with stinging nettle soup, then a fish course of mussels and other shellfish served with samphire. The main course could be wild pigeon and wild mushrooms with rowan jelly and sea beet. For dessert, bilberry tart, finishing off with chocolate sloes and dandelion coffee.

Above all, keep an open mind, experiment, and have fun.

Stinging Nettle

Spring

Surprisingly, perhaps, spring is actually a lean time for wild animals, whose autumn reserves have been used up, and fats, proteins and carbohydrates are in short supply.

For the wild food enthusiast, however, it is the time to take advantage of fresh new growth. Young leaves and shoots are at their tenderest, seaweeds at their peak, and there is the prospect of finding the first delicious Morels of the season.

◁ *Common Morel*

Hop

Gutweed

Sweet Violet

Primrose

Hop

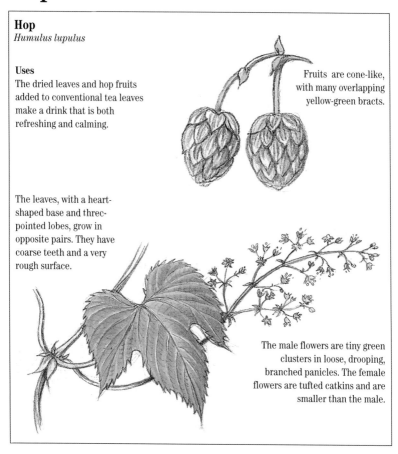

Hop
Humulus lupulus

Uses
The dried leaves and hop fruits added to conventional tea leaves make a drink that is both refreshing and calming.

Fruits are cone-like, with many overlapping yellow-green bracts.

The leaves, with a heart-shaped base and three-pointed lobes, grow in opposite pairs. They have coarse teeth and a very rough surface.

The male flowers are tiny green clusters in loose, drooping, branched panicles. The female flowers are tufted catkins and are smaller than the male.

Hedgerow and roadsides

Hop is a climbing plant that twines its way through hedgerows, along wire fences, up trees and up telegraph poles. It **is** famous for its use as a flavouring for beer: its bitter fruits were first used in this way in the Netherlands in the 14th Century; in Britain, the hop was resisted at first in favour of traditional plants such as Ground Ivy. In Hemp (*Cannabis sativa*) it has a close relative – but it shares none of Cannabis's well-known effects. Hop oil has soporific qualities, and the fruits are sometimes stuffed into pillows to aid sleep.

COOKING AND EATING Hop has provided food since Roman times, perhaps earlier: its young shoots were eaten like asparagus. They should be picked soon after they appear – no later than May. Soak them in salt water for a while to encourage any tiny insects to leave. Discard the older leaves, then chop the stems and fry gently in butter before adding to soups, omelettes or pasta dishes. Hopscotch, a dish from Kent, uses equal amounts of hops and Dandelion leaves sweated with onions in butter, seasoned with lemon juice, nutmeg, salt and pepper, and served with grilled bacon and mushrooms. The shoots may also be boiled for a few minutes until tender, and served with black pepper and hollandaise sauce.

Hop scrambles and clambers over hedges and fences, sometimes almost completely covering them with its pale string-like stems and hairy leaves. The observant may spot the characteristic leaves, which are very similar those of the grapevine, but the swollen fruits in late summer are unmistakable.

Hop

RANGE: Throughout Europe,except the far north.

HABITAT: Hedgerows and roadsides.

FLOWERING TIME: June to September. Fruits in late summer.

Stinging Nettle

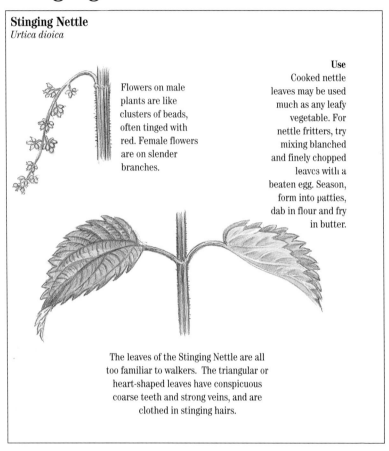

Stinging Nettle
Urtica dioica

Flowers on male plants are like clusters of beads, often tinged with red. Female flowers are on slender branches.

Use
Cooked nettle leaves may be used much as any leafy vegetable. For nettle fritters, try mixing blanched and finely chopped leaves with a beaten egg. Season, form into patties, dab in flour and fry in butter.

The leaves of the Stinging Nettle are all too familiar to walkers. The triangular or heart-shaped leaves have conspicuous coarse teeth and strong veins, and are clothed in stinging hairs.

Rough wasteland

Stinging Nettle is of course familiar to anyone who walks in the countryside, especially near farmland or waste ground. Sooner or later a leaf will brush against the skin, delivering its sting. There are stiff, hollow hairs on the surface of the leaf that are easily broken, and it is then that they release a fluid which is so irritating to human skin. There are also many non-stinging hairs – though the number varies from plant to plant. The tough stems are an excellent source of fibre, and have been used to make textiles said to be more durable than linen, which can, incidentally, be dyed green by the same plant.

COOKING AND EATING Surprisingly, young nettles are eminently edible, but must be gathered when no more than a few centimetres high. Wear gloves. They may be used as a substitute for spinach, cooked in no more water than clings to the leaves after washing. Nettle soup is a classic dish, and there are many variations: one of the tastiest is to make a simple potato and leek soup, with well seasoned stock and plenty of black pepper. Add the cooked nettle leaves with a little butter, and blend to a smooth consistency. Finish off with a little cream, and diced, grilled streaky bacon or lardons.

Stinging Nettle *grows to chest height, on stiff, erect stems, particularly on rich soils. However, the leaves should be gathered for eating while the plants are no more than knee-high. They are often found close to farmyard barns or field corners where the ground has been enriched by animals, or close to human habitation.*

Stinging Nettle

RANGE: Throughout the whole of Europe.

HABITAT: Rough wasteland.

FLOWERING TIME: May to September. The leaves should be gathered no later than June.

27

Common Sorrel

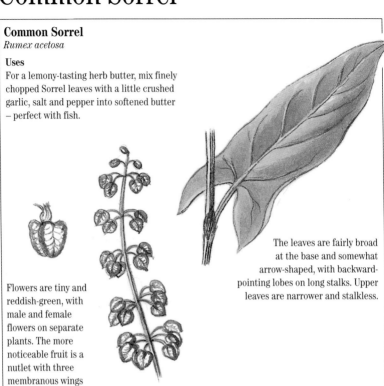

Common Sorrel
Rumex acetosa

Uses
For a lemony-tasting herb butter, mix finely
chopped Sorrel leaves with a little crushed
garlic, salt and pepper into softened butter
– perfect with fish.

The leaves are fairly broad
at the base and somewhat
arrow-shaped, with backward-
pointing lobes on long stalks. Upper
leaves are narrower and stalkless.

Flowers are tiny and
reddish-green, with
male and female
flowers on separate
plants. The more
noticeable fruit is a
nutlet with three
membranous wings
that turn red as they
develop (above).

Grassy meadows

Common Sorrel is one of those ubiquitous plants frequently ignored precisely because it is so common. It looks like a weed, and its flowers are somewhat insignificant, but a meadow tinted scarlet by its thin, erect stems laden with fruit makes a striking sight.

COOKING AND EATING The leaves contain oxalic acid and taste pleasantly sharp, so they make a useful addition to salads, soups and omelettes; or they can be cooked like spinach. Although most leaves of edible plants are best eaten when very young and tender, in the case of sorrel they can be left on the plant until the reddish fruit is mature, by which time the flavour has developed further.

For a delicious omelette, cook two good handfuls of washed Sorrel leaves, with the stalks discarded, in melted butter. Avoid using a metal pan or utensils, since the acid in the leaves can react with the metal and spoil the flavour. Meanwhile, beat 4 eggs with 1 tablespoon of cold water and season with salt and freshly ground pepper. Pour the eggs over the Sorrel and stir, lifting the edges occasionally to let the uncooked egg run underneath. When almost cooked through, fold the omelette in half: the residual heat will finish the job without allowing the omelette to become overcooked.

Common Sorrel *is an unprepossessing waist-high plant when viewed alone, but it transforms whole fields to a rich red colour when seen* en masse. *However, the distinctive arrow shape of the leaves is an aid to identifying the plant before the flowers are formed, or if the field has been mown for hay.*

Common Sorrel

RANGE: Throughout Europe.

HABITAT: Grassy meadows.

FLOWERING TIME: May and June.

29

Good King Henry

Good King Henry
Chenopodium bonus-henricus

Use
Cut some young shoots into 4 cm sections, and simmer in salted water until tender. Drain and wrap each section with slivers of smoked salmon. Dress with lemon juice and black pepper.

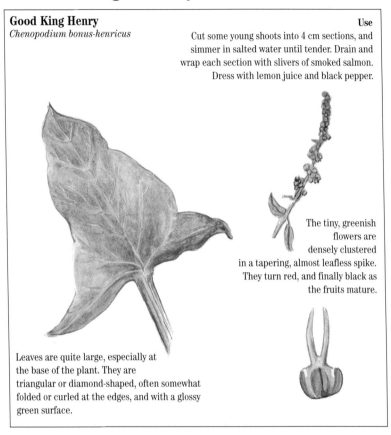

The tiny, greenish flowers are densely clustered in a tapering, almost leafless spike. They turn red, and finally black as the fruits mature.

Leaves are quite large, especially at the base of the plant. They are triangular or diamond-shaped, often somewhat folded or curled at the edges, and with a glossy green surface.

Farmland

This plant is a close relative of, and very similar to Fat Hen (page 220). They are both likely to be found in the same places, but Good King Henry has a liking for even richer soils, and is a perennial, producing a far greater abundance of edible material (especially from its second year onwards). It is most likely to be found on cultivated soils that have been manured, so allotments, farms and muck-heaps around stables are likely places in which to find it. Good King Henry was specifically grown as a cottage-garden crop, in some places in favour of spinach, and was much-loved in the sixteenth century, though it is now, undeservedly, thought of as a weed. Its unusual name refers not any particular monarch, but distinguishes it from another plant called Bad Henry – though it is unclear to which plant this ever referred.

COOKING AND EATING The leaves should be picked when reasonably young, and cooked in salted water like spinach, and may be added to pasta or omelettes. The shoots may also be collected, provided they are no more than 20 cm high or so, as they become too tough and bitter thereafter. They may be treated like asparagus, and used in flans such as quiche Lorriane, or cooked simply in garlic butter with salt and black pepper and enjoyed without the addition of anything else.

Good King Henry *grows from knee- to waist-height, but is perhaps the easiest of the goosefoot family to identify with its large, triangular leaves. It forms clumps or small patches of plants, usually on the most organically rich soils, and particularly where farmyard manure has been applied.*

Good King Henry

RANGE: Thoughout Europe except for the Iberian peninsula and northern Scandinavia.

HABITAT: Cultivated, rich soils.

FLOWERING TIME: May to August.

Sea Beet or Wild Spinach

Sea Beet or Wild Spinach
Beta vulgaris

Use
If cooking Mussels or Cockles over an open fire on the beach, be sure to throw some torn Sea Beet leaves in to the pot (there are bound to be some nearby), along with a generous splash of white wine.

Leaves are variable in shape, oval or spear-shaped, and have long stalks. They have a glossy green surface, sometimes tinged with red, and an almost leathery or fleshy texture. The leaves at the base of the plant can grow quite large.

The tiny green flowers are clustered in whorls to form a long, narrow spike, sometimes held erect or else prostrate over the ground. The stems are fleshy and ridged, often tinged with red.

Coast

Sea Beet is the ancestor not only of cultivated Beetroot, but also of such staple leafy vegetables as spinach and Swiss Chard. Unlike those cultivated varieties, wild Sea Beet prefers the poorest of soils, occurring on shingle beaches, sea walls and the drier parts of salt marshes. It is superficially similar to its relatives the goosefoots and oraches, of which there are several coastal varieties, but is distinguished because of its large glossy, fleshy leaves. Sea Beet may be harvested at any time from March to the first frosts, although the leaves are smallest during the flowering period in late summer. The big leaves are just as good as the small ones, but should be stripped of their stalks and midrib, which tend to be tough. They make a useful substitute for spinach, in flans or pasta dishes for example. They are not so good as a raw salad leaf however, being a little too robust, with a slight soapy taste.

COOKING AND EATING Try making this piquant relish for spreading on toast: gently fry two or three handfuls of chopped Sea Beet leaves in butter with some crushed garlic until well wilted. Squeeze out any liquid, blend with half a dozen anchovy fillets and 25g of softened butter, the juice of half a lemon, salt, pepper and nutmeg.

Sea Beet *forms prostrate tufts and clumps growing to knee-height or less, and often it is the only plant occupying the strand line of shingle beaches. Although the flowers are unremarkable, the clumps of erect flower spikes catch the sea breeze like sailing yachts in a regatta.*

Sea Beet

RANGE: European coasts except for Germany, Scandinavia and northern Scotland.

HABITAT: Shingle beaches, sea walls and salt marshes.

FLOWERING TIME: June to September.

33

Chickweed

Chickweed
Stellaria media

Uses
Folklore has it that an infusion of Chickweed is a remedy for obesity – unfortunately this is not founded in fact. Chickweed poultices were used to reduce swelling.

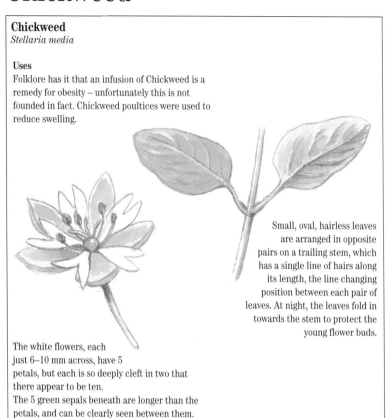

Small, oval, hairless leaves are arranged in opposite pairs on a trailing stem, which has a single line of hairs along its length, the line changing position between each pair of leaves. At night, the leaves fold in towards the stem to protect the young flower buds.

The white flowers, each just 6–10 mm across, have 5 petals, but each is so deeply cleft in two that there appear to be ten.
The 5 green sepals beneath are longer than the petals, and can be clearly seen between them.

Farmland

Chickweed is a very common plant of fields or disturbed ground, everywhere, and its cheerful tiny, starry flowers peer up towards the sky at almost any time of year – the long flowering period is typical of many successful plants. Chickweed appears in early spring and may be gathered any time until midsummer, when the leaves become rather coarse. It has a second flush in the autumn and will continue to grow if protected against frost. It is best harvested by snipping off the top growth with scissors to avoid pulling up the soil. It was frequently given to caged birds or chickens as a tonic and is much loved by wood pigeons. It has long been used as a tasty salad vegetable.

COOKING AND EATING   Chickweed is without bitterness and tastes a little like lettuce, and a delicious salad can be prepared with well-washed Chickweed, sliced ripe pears and flakes of parmesan. Add a little Hairy Bittercress and dress the salad with olive oil and balsamic vinegar. To make a delicious soup, fry a little onion in a saucepan, add some vegetable stock and a few potatoes. Boil until the potatoes are cooked, then throw in a couple of handfuls of Chickweed and cook for a further 5 minutes. Put the soup through a blender and season, before adding some single cream and finely sliced Ramsons leaves.

Chickweed *forms cushions of green between the crops in arable land, or creeps through long grass, producing pin-pricks of tiny white star-like flowers above bright green paired leaves. Do not confuse it with Common Mouse-ear (* Cerastium fontanum*), which has hairy, velvety leaves and a looser, more untidy appearance.*

Chickweed

RANGE: Throughout Europe.

HABITAT: Fields, farmyards cultivated and waste ground, shingle beaches.

FLOWERING TIME: All year, but mostly from March to November.

Hairy Bittercress

Hairy Bittercress
Cardamine hirsuta

Uses
The fresh young leaves have a mild, peppery taste,
not as strong as that of Watercress. Because of their
small size, it is best to gather just a few as a
flavouring for bulkier ingredients.

The leaves are mostly in a rosette at the
base, quite long and with rows of opposite,
rounded lobes. The stem produces small
ladder-like leaves.

The flowers are tiny and barely
noticeable, with 4 white petals,
and are over-topped by the
long seed-pods.

Rough wasteland

Hairy Bittercress is one of those plants that is easily overlooked, but can be found almost anywhere on farmland, on waste ground and in gardens, wherever the soil has been disturbed or there is little competition, including in pavement cracks and on old walls. The tiny white flowers are soon outgrown by the lengthening fruit capsules, which, when ripe, burst open at the slightest touch, audibly scattering the seeds some distance. The rosettes of ladder-like leaves are easily recognisable and easily found, even when the plant is quite young. Leaves should be gathered from sites where they will have avoided the attention of dogs, and well washed, since they tend to be a little dusty. Hairy Bittercress is available early in the spring, but may be found at any time of the year, except during the driest months.

COOKING AND EATING The tangy taste of the leaves complements the sweetness of soft ripe fruits beautifully. Prepare an exotic salad with lettuce (or another suitable wild salad vegetable, such as Chickweed) sliced ripe mango, avocado pear, chopped strawberries, a few basil leaves and a liberal handful of Hairy Bittercress leaves. Use a light dressing of lemon juice and sunflower oil.

36

Hairy Bittercress *is an almost insignificant weed of urban areas. It is short and slender, with the tiniest of flowers and long, thin seed-pods reaching upwards. The rosette of leaves, usually pressed close to the ground, and with rows of tiny, rounded leaflets on either side of the leaf-stalk, is more easily noticed than the flowers.*

Hairy Bittercress

RANGE: Throughout Europe, except the North.

HABITAT: Farmland, waste ground, gardens, where soil has been disturbed.

FLOWERING TIME: March to October.

Wood Sorrel

Wood Sorrel
Oxalis acetosella

Warning
The plant is a strong diuretic. It should not be consumed in
great quantities or by those suffering from rheumatism, gout
or kidney stones, since it may exacerbate these conditions.

The 5-petalled white flowers are
elegantly veined with pink, and
open only in good light. The small
sepals are greenish red.

Each delicate leaf is divided into
three leaflets, shaped rather like
those of clover, but they fold and
droop readily. They are held on thin,
unbranched, reddish stems.

Woodland

The delicate and curiously shaped leaves of Wood Sorrel are very
sensitive, drooping in strong sunshine to conserve moisture, or at
night folding along the length of each leaflet, like a closed umbrella.
The flowers are equally delicate, and the plant tends to form dainty
patches within woodland, rather than great swathes. It is equally at
home in coniferous or deciduous woods, and is often to be found at the mossy base of a
tree trunk. Although the flowering period is short, the leaves are instantly recognizable
and are available for a much longer period. They have a sharp, invigorating acid taste, with
a hint of lemon, due to a high oxalic acid content. Both parts of the scientific name reflect
this: the Greek *Oxys* means acid, and *acetosella* means vinegar salts, and a few popped
in the mouth are a refreshing pick-me-up on a woodland walk.

COOKING AND EATING Small quantities of the refreshing leaves may be used to
enliven salads; the flowers, too, make a decorative, though largely flavourless,
addition. If the leaves are cooked and used in soups or sauces, the oxalic acid content
is reduced, but some flavour remains. As an accompaniment to fish, cook 1 cup of
Wood Sorrel leaves in 50g butter, whisk in 1 cup of single cream, season and heat.

Wood Sorrel *is instantly recognizable by its little triad of bright yellow-green folded leaves, usually over the leaf litter of a woodland floor. The cheerful pink-veined flowers are conspicuous, but are not open for very long, although the leaves remain present well into the summer.*

Wood Sorrel

Range: Throughout Europe.

Habitat: Coniferous and deciduous woodland.

Flowering Time: April to June.

Sweet Violet

Sweet Violet
Viola odorata

Use
For a great personalised gift, steep a generous handful of violet flowers in some white wine vinegar, which will take on a brilliant purple tint and sweet odour.

Leaves are in basal tufts, with a fairly rounded or kidney-shaped outline, and a bluntly-toothed edge.

The flowers have 5 violet or purple petals, white in the centre, with dark purple lines, and a pouch or spur at the back which is also purple. Sometimes white flowers with a pink spur occur.

Hedgerows, roadsides

There are many species of violet, often difficult to separate, but this one is perhaps the most widely distributed. The first clue to identifying Sweet Violet is its flowering time, which may be as early as February. Purple (very occasionally white) flowers peer through the rounded leaves and continue to multiply throughout the summer. The flower has a sweet scent and has been cultivated not only for cut flowers but also for making a syrup by boiling them up with sugar. The springtime flowers only rarely set seed, as there are few pollinating insects at that time. A second crop of special flowers is produced in the autumn. These have no petals, and do not open fully. The plant self-fertilizes, and can produce seed, although it also spreads by creeping stems.

COOKING AND EATING In spite of the lack of insects to pollinate them, the springtime flowers are full of nectar. An ideal way to make use of this surplus is to make crystalllized violets for cake decoration. Beat some egg white until frothy, but not stiff. Carefully pull the flowers away from their green sepals, dip them in the egg white and dust liberally with icing sugar. Allow to dry on kitchen paper for 24 hours in a cool place. They will keep for several weeks in a sealed jar in the refrigerator.

Sweet Violet *is one of the first of the shade-loving plants to appear in spring. The rounded pale green leaves, often quite large and overlapping one another, are instantly recognizable. The purple flowers are usually abundant only on younger plants.*

Sweet Violet

RANGE: Throughout Europe, except the far north.

HABITAT: Semi-shaded spots alongside woods, hedgerows and paths.

FLOWERING TIME: February to May.

Cow Parsley

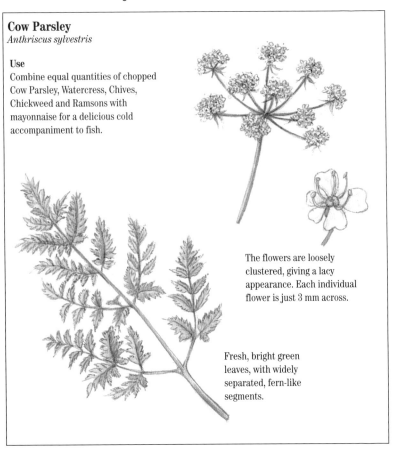

Cow Parsley
Anthriscus sylvestris

Use
Combine equal quantities of chopped Cow Parsley, Watercress, Chives, Chickweed and Ramsons with mayonnaise for a delicious cold accompaniment to fish.

The flowers are loosely clustered, giving a lacy appearance. Each individual flower is just 3 mm across.

Fresh, bright green leaves, with widely separated, fern-like segments.

Hedgerows, roadsides

Swathes of tall white flowers along roadsides and through open woods in May are likely to be those of Cow Parsley. They appear like great waves of foam, and indicate that spring is well and truly established. The leaves often appear as early as December in mild climates, and a few plants may flower earlier than the mass showing which is so familiar. It is imperative not to confuse this plant with the fatally poisonous Hemlock (*Conium maculatum*), which is taller and has more finely divided leaves and red-spotted stems, or the shorter Fool's Parsley (*Arethusa cynapium*), which has long bracts drooping down from the flower-heads.

COOKING AND EATING Cow Parsley is closely related to the herb Chervil, and can be used in its place. It has a cool, refreshing aftertaste and, used sparingly, goes well with fish. Quickly fry some mackerel fillets in a little butter – there is nothing like the taste of freshly caught mackerel – remove them and deglaze the pan with half a glass of white wine. Boil rapidly to reduce this stock, then whisk in a knob of butter. Squeeze in a little lemon juice and add some chopped Cow Parsley leaves, salt and black pepper. Pour over the fish and serve with new potatoes, green beans or carrots.

Cow Parsley *produces masses of frothy white flowers along roadsides in spring, usually waist- to shoulder-high and with an open, spreading habit. It is by far the most common roadside member of the carrot family, but watch out for the lookalikes Hemlock and Fool's Parsley.*

Cow Parsley

RANGE: Throughout Europe.

HABITAT: Hedgerows and roadsides.

FLOWERING TIME: April to June.

Ground Elder

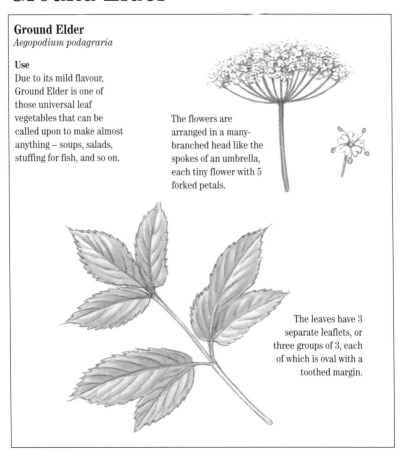

Ground Elder
Aegopodium podagraria

Use
Due to its mild flavour, Ground Elder is one of those universal leaf vegetables that can be called upon to make almost anything – soups, salads, stuffing for fish, and so on.

The flowers are arranged in a many-branched head like the spokes of an umbrella, each tiny flower with 5 forked petals.

The leaves have 3 separate leaflets, or three groups of 3, each of which is oval with a toothed margin.

Woodland

Ground Elder is a plant much feared by gardeners, for it is a persistent weed of shady places and woodland edges that increases by underground spreading roots, the smallest fragment of which can give rise to a new colony. In former times it was encouraged to grow near human habitation, as the leaves were eaten like spinach, and it was cultivated by monks as a cure for gout (the name *podagraria* comes from the Latin *podagra*, meaning gout). In spite of the bad reputation it now has, Ground Elder is an attractive plant when in flower, with rounded clusters of white blooms held just above the dense covering of mid-green leaves, which bear a resemblance to those of Elder.

COOKING AND EATING The young leaves appear from May onwards, but can be encouraged to keep growing right through to the first frosts if cut regularly. Their flavour is mild but pleasant; the stalks in particular have a hint of celery. For a delicious spring or summer salad, mix up some sliced apple, roughly chopped walnuts, Ground Elder leaves and stalks, and cubes of sheeps-milk cheese. Dress with olive oil, lemon juice, salt and pepper. Alternatively, wash some young leaves and cook them in a covered pan with just a knob of butter for a couple of minutes, until soft. Serve with lots of black pepper.

Ground Elder *colonizes shady areas with a dense covering of three-part leaves at about knee-height or less, and produces rounded heads of white flowers on taller stems. It is a rapidly invasive plant, the scourge of gardeners and the prize of cooks.*

Ground Elder

RANGE: Throughout Europe, except the far north.

HABITAT: Shady places and woodland edge.

FLOWERING TIME: May to July.

45

Common Comfrey

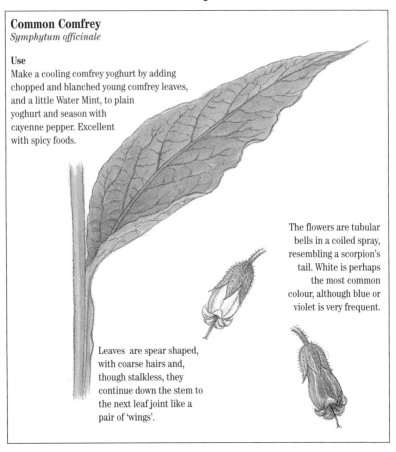

Common Comfrey
Symphytum officinale

Use
Make a cooling comfrey yoghurt by adding chopped and blanched young comfrey leaves, and a little Water Mint, to plain yoghurt and season with cayenne pepper. Excellent with spicy foods.

The flowers are tubular bells in a coiled spray, resembling a scorpion's tail. White is perhaps the most common colour, although blue or violet is very frequent.

Leaves are spear shaped, with coarse hairs and, though stalkless, they continue down the stem to the next leaf joint like a pair of 'wings'.

Ponds, ditches

The hanging bell-shaped flowers of Common Comfrey may be blue, pink or white, and open in sequence from the base to the tip. It grows in damp places, such as river and stream margins, wet woodland and damp meadows. The plant has a long history of use for various ailments, chief of them being its apparent ability to speed up the mending of broken bones. *Symphytum* comes from the Greek, *sympho* – to unite. Modern research has shown that the plant contains allantoin, a substance proven to accelerate the healing process by causing cells to multiply more quickly. Russian Comfrey (*Symphytum* x *uplandicum*) is a frequently seen hybrid, which usually has blue flowers and shorter wings down the stems.

COOKING AND EATING Only the young and tender leaves should be picked for eating. Comfrey fritters are a classic dish: make a batter by mixing 100 g plain flour, salt, pepper, an egg and 150 ml sparkling mineral water (the bubbles help to lighten the mixture, but stir gently to avoid removing them). Dip some comfrey leaves, complete with stalks, into the batter one by one and deep fry them in hot oil until golden brown – about 2 minutes should be enough. Drain on kitchen paper and serve with comfrey yoghurt.

Common Comfrey is a robust plant growing waist- to chest-height. It is very leafy, but dotted with pendent bells of blue, violet, white or pink. It loves to grow in damp places, but is also grown in cottage gardens for its efficacy in helping to heal wounds and mend broken bones.

Common Comfrey

RANGE: Throughout Europe, except the far north.

HABITAT: River and stream margins, wet woodland, damp meadows.

FLOWERING TIME: May to July.

Primrose

Primrose
Primula vulgaris

Uses
The young leaves may be used in salad, as
may the flowers, but avoid picking too
many from wild plants since they are
becoming rare in some areas. Better still,
grow the wild form in the garden to
ensure a steady supply.

The flowers all arise from
the base on long stalks, but
there is only one flower to a
stalk, with 5 notched pale
yellow petals and deeper
yellow spots in the centre.

The leaves also all arise from the base.
They are oblong, tapering towards the
base, and have a very wrinkled surface
like old leather, and a pale mid-rib.

Hedgerows, woodland

Mild weather may see Primroses flowering as early as December in
isolated pockets, but the main show begins in February and March.
They prefer slightly damp rich soils, and though most often seen in open
woodland or hedgerows, may turn up in surprising locations such as new
motorway verges. Two types of flower are produced, always on separate
plants, in which the anthers and stigma occupy different positions so
that cross-fertilization is assured when they are visited by long-tongued bees.

COOKING AND EATING Primrose flowers, and those of the closely related Cowslip, were
used for making wine. The tiny amount of nectar at the base of the petals gave the wine its
flavour, so vast quantities were needed to have any appreciable effect. Such harvesting
would wreak havoc on the countryside in modern times, but a few may be collected for
crystallizing. Follow the recipe for crystallizing violets on page 40, and use them to decorate
a Victoria sponge for Easter. Cream 150 g sugar with 150 g butter, then mix in 3 eggs and
150 g self-raising flour. Pour into two greased 18 cm cake tins and bake for 25 minutes at
170°C. When cool, spread one half with strawberry jam, sandwich it with the other, cover
with a thin layer of icing and decorate with the Primrose flowers.

Primroses *form a natural posy of fresh green leaves and the loveliest of clean, unsullied flowers that sum up the essence of springtime. Occasionally flowers of different colours can occur, typically orange, pink or brown: usually the result of breeding with plants that have escaped from cultivation.*

Primrose

RANGE: Southern and western Europe.

HABITAT: Open woodland, along hedgerows.

FLOWERING TIME: February to May, though sometimes even earlier.

Tansy

Tansy
Tanacetum vulgare

Use
Since they are strong in flavour, it is best to gather only the youngest leaves for culinary use, and they should, even then, be used in moderation.

The flowers are a dense collection of disc florets, forming a tight rounded 'button' with a flat top. Several of the 'buttons' are concentrated together in a cluster.

The leaves are divided into many opposite, narrow lobes which are sharply toothed, like the frond of a fern.

Tansy is a tall, attractive herb, easily identified by its clusters of golden buttons, though the fern-like leaves are also characteristic. It has a history of use as a strewing herb – spread about the house to repel insects. When grown with fruit trees, it can also keep away pests.

Hedgerows, roadsides   It has also been used as a tea to expel intestinal worms, but the leaves do contain some toxin and so regular or excessive use is considered dangerous. The plant thrives on a variety of soils, but is most often seen on roadsides, on disturbed wasteground, or cultivated fields.

COOKING AND EATING   Traditionally, Tansy was used at Easter in various kinds of omelette or pancake, but the leaves are not always available so early in the year. It was also used as a general substitute for expensive spices, but the flavour is extremely hot and pungent by today's standards and may not be to everyone's taste. To make a traditional tansy pancake, make a rich batter of 100 g flour, 300 ml cream, 3 eggs and 1 tablespoon of sugar; add grated orange rind, 4 teaspoons of chopped tansy leaves, 1 tablespoon of melted butter and a slug of sherry. Leave to stand for half an hour, fry the pancakes in a little butter and serve with orange slices.

Tansy *grows chest- height or taller, with flat tops of densely clustered golden coins above a mass of fern-like leaves. It often forms considerable colonies along the roadside. It used to be a staple of cottage gardens so that the leaves could be used as a spice, but the flavour is very strong.*

Tansy

RANGE: Throughout Europe.

HABITAT: Roadsides, wasteground, cultivated fields.

FLOWERING TIME: July to September.

Ramsons

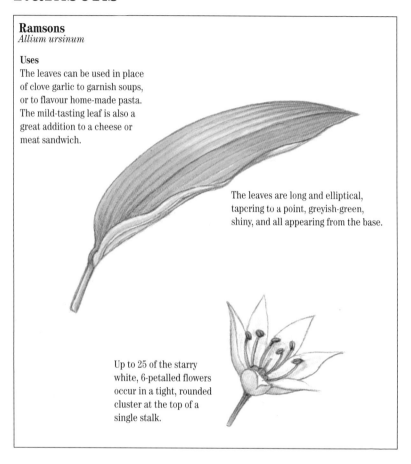

Ramsons
Allium ursinum

Uses
The leaves can be used in place of clove garlic to garnish soups, or to flavour home-made pasta. The mild-tasting leaf is also a great addition to a cheese or meat sandwich.

The leaves are long and elliptical, tapering to a point, greyish-green, shiny, and all appearing from the base.

Up to 25 of the starry white, 6-petalled flowers occur in a tight, rounded cluster at the top of a single stalk.

Woodland

Ramsons is a member of the onion family, and may form great carpets over a large area in damp woodland or shady banks in spring, often to the exclusion of other plants, although in the mild climates of the far west it appears out in the open among rocks. The scent of the leaves and flowers can be almost overpowering on warm, still days, but the taste of the leaves is milder than their fragrance suggests.

COOKING AND EATING This plant is somewhat milder than clove garlic and the delicate-tasting leaves are great in salads. Alternatively, a fresh pesto can be made, using the leaves combined with olive oil, pine or hazel nuts and parmesan cheese. It provides a tasty accompaniment to pasta.

The mild taste lends itself to fish dishes and is especially good with Sea Bass. With a sharp knife, make three or four incisions on both sides of the fish, place ten or so fresh Ramsons leaves with a couple of knobs of butter in the cavity, brush with olive oil and place in a shallow dish. Cover it loosely with foil and bake the fish in a medium oven for 25–35 minutes, according to size. Serve with new potatoes sprinkled with chopped parsley and lemon wedges.

***Ramsons** forms swathes of slightly fleshy, greyish leaves in spring, followed by rounded 'pom-pons' of starry flowers like white lollipops, which fill the air with a heady garlic scent. They may be found in deciduous woods or on shady hedge banks, but only where these have been undisturbed for many years.*

Ramsons

RANGE: Western Europe.

HABITAT: Damp woodland.

FLOWERING TIME:
About three weeks between late April and early June.
The leaves are available for most of this period.

Green Seaweeds

Green Seaweeds

Sea Lettuce
Ulva lactuca
Easily recognized for its clusters of thin, broad, leaf-like fronds, bearing a strong resemblance to lettuce. They are usually pale green and semi-translucent, but looking a little like cooked spinach when lying flat on the rocks when the tide has gone out.

Gutweed
Enteromorpha intestinalis
The fronds are long, thin hollow tubes, only 20 mm wide and usually about 30 cm long, but sometimes much longer. At intervals they are partly filled with air sacs, giving them the unappetising appearance of a portion of bright, grassy-green intestine. Gutweed is attached by a tiny disc to rocks and stones.

Coast

Green seaweeds are among the simplest of all plants, reproducing by spores. Their tissues are not clearly differentiated into roots, stems or leaves. Eating Seaweed is not natural to the modern European palate, but some seaside communities have eaten it from time immemorial. Perhaps the current popularity of Oriental cuisine will increase interest in it too. Of the two species illustrated, Gutweed is the least attractive, bearing a close resemblance to an alarmingly-coloured digestive tract, but it is delicious, especially if the texture is transformed by the cooking method below.

COOKING AND EATING Gutweed is very common on the upper tidal zone in rock pools. Gather a few fronds and wash them well in fresh water, draining well and patting dry with kitchen paper. Stir fry them in hot vegetable oil in a wok for a few minutes until crisp, and dress with soy sauce, lime juice and brown sugar. Sea Lettuce is also common on the upper tidal zone, near places where fresh water drains into the sea (take care that such places are not sewage outlets). Toss the fronds in butter and dress with a cream, oil and lemon juice sauce, well-seasoned with black pepper. Or, cut them into pieces and serve as a salad with a horseradish and vinegar sauce and mackerel pieces.

Gutweed forms tangles of long, stringy masses clinging to rocks and stones on the upper tidal zone. Do not be put off by its odd appearance.

Green Seaweeds

RANGE: Both are common throughout the region in the Mediterranean, Atlantic, English Channel, North Sea and Baltic.

COLLECTING PERIOD: Spring to early summer, when the fronds are young.

Brown Seaweeds

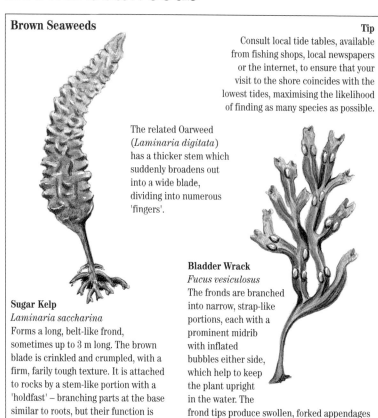

Brown Seaweeds

Tip
Consult local tide tables, available from fishing shops, local newspapers or the internet, to ensure that your visit to the shore coincides with the lowest tides, maximising the likelihood of finding as many species as possible.

The related Oarweed (*Laminaria digitata*) has a thicker stem which suddenly broadens out into a wide blade, dividing into numerous 'fingers'.

Bladder Wrack
Fucus vesiculosus
The fronds are branched into narrow, strap-like portions, each with a prominent midrib with inflated bubbles either side, which help to keep the plant upright in the water. The frond tips produce swollen, forked appendages which are the reproductive parts.

Sugar Kelp
Laminaria saccharina
Forms a long, belt-like frond, sometimes up to 3 m long. The brown blade is crinkled and crumpled, with a firm, fairly tough texture. It is attached to rocks by a stem-like portion with a 'holdfast' – branching parts at the base similar to roots, but their function is solely to attach to the plant.

Coast

Brown Seaweeds are algae whose green chlorophyll is masked by the presence of a brown pigment called fucoxanthin. They are commonest in cold, northern waters. Sugar Kelp is a familiar and easily recognised seaweed of the lower tidal zone, often exposed only at the lowest tides, though fronds are frequently washed ashore higher up. When Sugar Kelp dries, small crystals of a sugary substance, mannitol, appear on the surface. Try to collect young fronds, cutting the stems just below the blades and leaving the holdfast intact, so that they can re-grow.

COOKING AND EATING Wash the fronds well and hang up in a warm place indoors to dry them out, when they will become rather crispy. Cut these into small squares and fry quickly for a few seconds in hot oil. Drain and sprinkle with salt. The salt and natural sugariness makes them an ideal 'nibble' to serve with drinks. Bladder Wrack usually occurs in the mid tidal zone. Like many seaweeds, the fronds contain alginates, a natural thickener, which makes them ideal for adding to soups and stews. Several other similar species occur without the gas-filled bladders: Toothed Wrack (*F. serratus*) has fronds with serrated margins, and Spiral Wrack (*F. spiralis*) has twisted fronds.

Bladder Wrack *forms extensive beds but in a well-defined area in the mid tidal zone shore, the fronds lying over the rocks in vast quantities, often to the exclusion of other seaweeds.*

Brown Seaweeds

RANGE: Both common in the Atlantic, English Channel and North Sea.

COLLECTING PERIOD: Available all year, but best in spring when young.

Red Seaweeds

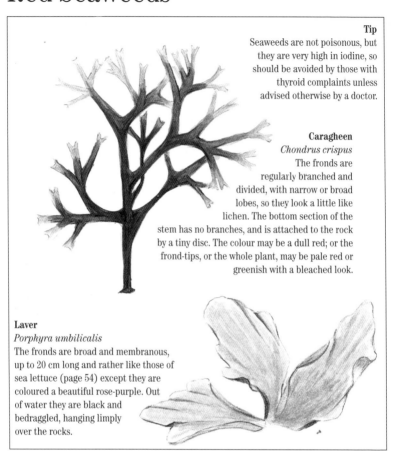

Tip
Seaweeds are not poisonous, but they are very high in iodine, so should be avoided by those with thyroid complaints unless advised otherwise by a doctor.

Caragheen
Chondrus crispus
The fronds are regularly branched and divided, with narrow or broad lobes, so they look a little like lichen. The bottom section of the stem has no branches, and is attached to the rock by a tiny disc. The colour may be a dull red; or the frond-tips, or the whole plant, may be pale red or greenish with a bleached look.

Laver
Porphyra umbilicalis
The fronds are broad and membranous, up to 20 cm long and rather like those of sea lettuce (page 54) except they are coloured a beautiful rose-purple. Out of water they are black and bedraggled, hanging limply over the rocks.

Coast

Many Red Seaweeds grow in deep water below the tide line, as they can survive in low levels of light. However, both these species may be found on the middle and lower areas of the tidal zone. They may lose their colour where exposed to strong light, appearing bleached or greenish. Carragheen, in particular, is very high in alginates which act like gelatine, and so can be used to make jellies and blancmanges. It dries well, so can be kept almost indefinitely and used when required.

COOKING AND EATING Use 5 g of dried carragheen to 500 ml of milk, soaking the carragheen in cold water first for 15 minutes to rehydrate it. Then simmer in the milk for 15-25 minutes until the milk really thickens, and add an egg yolk. The whisked egg white can be folded in to lighten the mixture before leaving it to set in the fridge. The mixture can be either sweetened with sugar and fruit, or made savoury with, for example, seasoning, herbs, or fish paste. Laver has a traditional use in seaside communities. The washed fronds are boiled or steamed until they break up into a black, mushy purée (this can take hours). Traditionally, the purée, called laver bread, is rolled in oatmeal and fried, or can be spread on to toast. Laver can also be added to soup.

Carragheen *is common and widespread in the lower tidal zone, more or less retaining its branched, firm structure even when out of the water.*

Red Seaweeds

RANGE: Both are common in the Atlantic, English Channel and North Sea.

COLLECTING PERIOD: Available all year, but best in spring when young.

Common Morel

Common Morel

Morchella esculenta

Head with deep polygonal cavities; hollow stem; appears in spring

Use

Morels dry particularly well if threaded on to a string and hung up in a warm place. Always clean them thoroughly – insects and debris find their way into the small cavities.

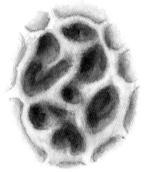

Cap variable in form, from almost spherical to ovoid or conical, yellow, yellowish brown to blackish brown, and bearing deep ridges with cross walls to give a honeycomb-like appearance of polygonal cavities, hollow

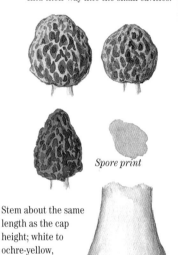

Spore print

Stem about the same length as the cap height; white to ochre-yellow, smooth or scurfy, sometimes ribbed or wrinkled, hollow

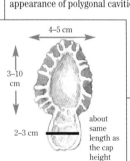

4–5 cm

3–10 cm

2–3 cm

about same length as the cap height

Once established, the Morel often reappears at the same site for many years. It is much prized as a spring-time fun gus, appearing for just a short time in March or April, and for its eating qualities. It is very variable, both in colour and shape, and may often have a dark conical head. It is important not to confuse it with the poisonous Turban Fungus or 'false morel', which is like a brain, with soft rounded convolutions and without polygonal cavities.

COOKING AND EATING Morels should always be cooked, never eaten raw. The flavour is too good to require much adornment, so they are best cooked simply and without mixing with other species They are excellent fried in butter then added to a rich white sauce with a little brandy, for pouring over fillet steak. They are also superb mixed with scrambled egg, served on a bed of Chickweed or Dandelion leaves. For a quick snack, sautée a shallot in a little olive oil until soft. Add some Morels, and red or yellow peppers, cut into strips. Cook for 5 minutes, and season with salt, pepper and nutmeg. Pour in a slug of white wine, and when the wine has reduced by half, throw in a handful of fresh Sorrel leaves and allow them to just wilt before serving.

Habitat: *On bare, sandy ground, under hedgerows, on embankments and roadsides, generally where there is little competition, usually in groups, sometimes in very large numbers.*

LOOKALIKES

Turban Fungus
Gyromitra esculenta A conifer-wood species, especially under pines and spruce, having a much-lobed, brain-like, reddish brown cap and short, whitish stalk. Poisonous; deadly if eaten raw and sometimes harmful even after cooking.

Turban Fungus

Common White Saddle
Helvella crispa Common species with a whitish, convoluted, saddle-shaped cap, 2-5 cm across, and deeply furrowed, whitish stalk; in woodlands from July to October. Edible but worthless.

Common White Saddle

Elfin Saddle
Helvella lacunosa Similar in form, but has dark grey or blackish cap and stem, and lobes of the cap attached to the stem in places.

St George's Mushroom

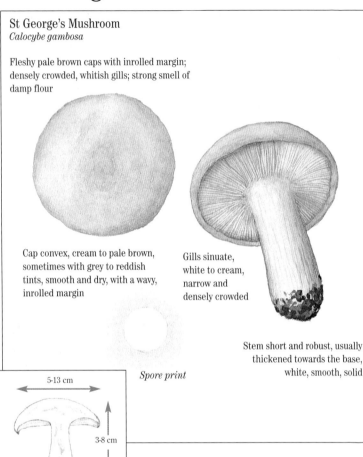

St George's Mushroom
Calocybe gambosa

Fleshy pale brown caps with inrolled margin;
densely crowded, whitish gills; strong smell of
damp flour

Cap convex, cream to pale brown,
sometimes with grey to reddish
tints, smooth and dry, with a wavy,
inrolled margin

Gills sinuate,
white to cream,
narrow and
densely crowded

Spore print

Stem short and robust, usually
thickened towards the base,
white, smooth, solid

5-13 cm

3-8 cm

1-2.5 cm

St George's Mushroom is one of the few wild, edible mushrooms of spring: its English name derives from its appearance on St George's Day (23 April). It was well known as an edible mushroom to the Ancient Romans. Due to its early appearance, it is unlikely to be confused with other species, but beware the lookalikes shown opposite. It has a very distinctive and rather strong, mealy smell of newly ground flour, which once experienced is never forgotten. Usually, several are found growing together.

COOKING AND EATING The fairly thick and robust flesh cooks well without becoming mushy. Cook some mushrooms in butter for a few minues until they turn golden brown. In a separate pan, fry a fillet of trout in a little sunflower oil until just cooked through; season with salt and pepper. The delicate flavours of this quick, simple dish are best appreciated without a sauce.

Habitat: *Large fairy rings in grassland, preferring chalky soils, in the spring.*

LOOKALIKES

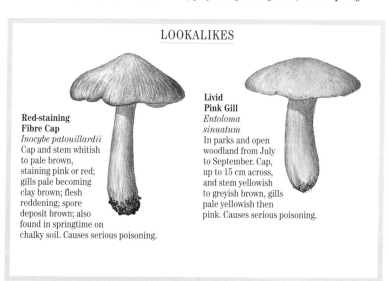

Red-staining Fibre Cap
Inocybe patouillardii
Cap and stem whitish to pale brown, staining pink or red; gills pale becoming clay brown; flesh reddening; spore deposit brown; also found in springtime on chalky soil. Causes serious poisoning.

Livid Pink Gill
Entoloma sinuatum
In parks and open woodland from July to September. Cap, up to 15 cm across, and stem yellowish to greyish brown, gills pale yellowish then pink. Causes serious poisoning.

Fairy Ring Champignon

Fairy Ring Champignon

Marasmius oreades

Many fruitbodies in fairy rings; cap and stem buffy brown, gills widely spaced

Uses
Eat soon after picking, with light summery foods such as salad or eggs. These mushrooms dry well, and can be kept for years and added to casseroles; drying is said to improve the flavour.

Cap at first bell-shaped finally flattening, although often with a raised centre and a wavy margin, pale buffy brown but drying much paler, dry, smooth

Spore print

Gills adnexed, white, broad, widely spaced

2-5 cm

2-7 cm

0.2-0.4 cm

Stem thin, tough, dry, similarly coloured to cap

Fairy Ring Champignon fruitbodies can appear very suddenly after heavy rain. Although it can be easily collected in enormous numbers, care must be taken to avoid picking the poisonous cream clot, which can grow in the same situation and can be intermixed. It is unpopular with gardeners: the fairy rings it tends to form can be large and last for many years.

COOKING AND EATING It is a good edible mushroom, with smell reminiscent of hay. It has a delicate texture and flavour – it tastes slightly of flour – and thin flesh, so should not be overcooked. One quick and simple, yet impressive, recipe uses duck breasts. Brush one side of the duck breasts with honey and grill for 10 minutes until the honey caramelizes, turn over and do the other side. Allow the breasts to rest for 5–10 minutes, while you quickly fry some Fairy Ring Champignons, stalks removed, in olive oil with a little garlic. Prepare a salad bed of Chickweed, Cornsalad, Dandelion, Hairy Bittercress, or other available leaves. Slice the breasts no more than 1 cm thick, and place warm on the salad with the mushrooms. Finish off with black pepper, a sprinkling of chopped Wood Sorrel leaves and a yoghurt, oil and vinegar dressing.

Habitat: *Grows in large numbers in grassland, especially on lawns, where it frequently forms extensive, perennial fairy rings.*

LOOKALIKES

Cream Clot

Silky Pink Gill

Silky Pink Gill
Entoloma sericea
Grows in troops amongst grass. Cap 2–4 cm across, dark sepia brown, drying silky; gills pink; stem slender, greyish brown. Inedible and may be confused with other poisonous pink gills.

Cream Clot
Clitocybe dealbata Cap, stem and gills white; gills short decurrent and crowded; spore deposit white. Sometimes grows with the Fairy Ring Champignon. Very poisonous.

Cracking Funnel Cap
Clitocybe rivulosa
Similar to the cream clot but cap white with small, pinkish patches, often cracking. Also in grassland. Poisonous.

Summer

The season of new abundance, and fresh opportunities. Many of the spring-growth leaves and shoots are still available, and there are also new flavours to explore. The first of the summer fruits are beginning to ripen. Now is the time for picking Lime flowers, Elderflowers or Meadowsweet for refreshing drinks on hot afternoons, and the time to go to the coast for prawns or shrimps, cooked over a beach fire at sunset, with a side dish of Samphire.

◁ *Meadowsweet*

Rock Samphire

Poppy

Borage

Chanterelle

Common Lime

Common Lime
Tilia europea

Leaves alternate on the shoot, a rounded egg shape to a triangular egg shape, 3-8 cm by 3-8 cm. Apex has an abrupt, slender point, base is oblique and deeply heart shaped Margin has regular, sharp teeth. Upper surface matt and somewhat bluish green, underside bluish with red or orange tufts (axils) in the junction of the veins. Leaf stalk 2-4 cm.

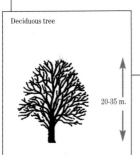

Shoot green and soon without hairs. Buds bluntly pointed, green with only two protective scales showing.

Deciduous tree

20-35 m.

Use

The leaves of all Limes may be used as a sandwich filling, provided that they are young, before the flowers have formed.

Flowers fragrant and whitish cream in July. Held level, with or above the leaves, in clusters of five to 11 with a large, leafy bract.

Fruit oval to round, smooth, with a thin shell. No ridges.

SIMILAR SPECIES
Tilia platyphyllos
Leaves of Large-leaved Lime are a broad egg shape and larger than Small-leaved Lime's, 6-15 cm by 7-13 cm. They have a dense covering of simple hairs on both surfaces.

Small-leaved Lime (*Tilia cordata*) and Large-leaved Lime (*Tilia platyphyllos*) both occur naturally throughout Europe except for the far north and Spain. They have been managed in woodlands as coppiced trees – cut down to ground level every few years and allowed to sprout. The stumps can be 6 m across and perhaps 2,000 years old, although in such large stumps the centre rots away leaving an incomplete ring of stems. Coppicing was carried out partly for the wood, but more especially for the bark. This was stripped off the stems and rotted, leaving the fibres, which were twisted into rope. More common than either of the two species these days is the hybrid between them, Common Lime (*Tilia europaea*), which is very often planted as a street tree or in avenues. The leaves are fairly large and have brown tufts of hair in the vein-axils underneath. The huge numbers of aphids living on the leaves produce a sugary substance, honeydew, which rains on anything underneath making it very sticky.

COOKING AND EATING The flowers of all Limes are sweetly scented, and make a honey-scented green tea that soothes the nervous and digestive systems. Pick the flowers at their most fresh, and dry them in a warm room for two weeks.

Common Lime is the species most likely to be encountered: by roadsides, parks, churchyards and gardens. It forms a tall, billowing crown, and often has an excess of basal suckers. The flowers of all three species are similar.

BARK
Dull grey to dark brown, fissured or with shallow ridges and often interrupted with large burrs or bosses.

Wild Cherry

Wild Cherry
Prunus avium

Fruit (2 cm) ripens in mid summer. It is round, with a juicy covering over the hard, bony seed, ripening to blackish red or yellow-red.

Tip
It is often necessary to gather cherries from the tree before they are fully ripe, and then ripen them in a warm place at home, otherwise the birds will get them all.

Leaves alternate on the shoot, oblong to oval, 7-12 cm by 4-5 cm, folded along the mid vein when young. Tip has a slender point. The base is rounded or wedge shaped, and the margin has sharp saw teeth. Upper surface dark green; underside paler, with hairs on the raised veins. Leaf stalk 2-3.5 cm, with two to five stalked glands.

Shoot is shiny purple brown, with bluntly pointed egg-shaped buds, 0.5 cm long.

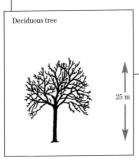

White flowers in mid spring in small clusters with the new foliage, hanging down, 2.5-3.5 cm.

Deciduous tree

25 m

The Wild Cherry is native throughout Europe except for the far north, and is the parent tree for the sweet cherry varieties used in orchards worldwide. The tree grows on a range of soils, but on dry, sandy ones it tends to be short lived. The largest trees develop on moisture-retentive clays or loams, and can be nearly as big as Oak in mixed woodland. The hard, light red timber is excellent, used for furniture, flooring and sculpture; and fetches a higher price than Oak. The fruit can be either sweet or bitter, though it is not sharp, so the amount of sugar needed when preparing it can only be determined by tasting.

COOKING AND EATING A surprisingly delicious use for them, popular in Eastern Europe, is Wild Cherry soup. Put 500 g of stoned and de-stalked cherries in a pan (do not use aluminium, as it can taint the flavour). Add a whole bottle (750 ml) of light red wine, a little ground cinnamon, and 100-200 g of granulated sugar, depending on the bitterness of the cherries. Simmer for ten minutes and allow to cool. Then liquidize the cherry mixture in a blender until smooth, and press it through a sieve to remove any lumps. Now stir in 500 ml of crème fraiche and 30 ml of kirsch. Taste the soup, adding more caster sugar or lemon juice as necessary. Chill for two hours before serving.

Wild Cherry makes a very attractive sight in spring when in full flower and can brighten mixed woodland, orchards or gardens. Branches of young trees are in spaced whorls; on older trees, the crown is rounded, dense and twiggy.

BARK
Shiny, purplish red and peeling slightly in young trees. There are prominent breathing pores (lenticels). Older trees develop grey or black fissures.

Plum

Plum
Prunus domestica

Flowers, up to 2.5 cm across, have five white petals, borne singly or in clusters of up to three. They appear before the leaves on rather dark, knobbly twigs.

Use
Make a quick Plum sauce by boiling the stoned and chopped fruit for a few minutes with a little red wine, brown sugar and ground cumin, until reduced to a thick, pouring consistency. Strain through a sieve and serve with duck or game.

Leaves arranged alternately. They are oval, though often wider towards the end, and have finely toothed margins. Usually matt green in colour.

The fruit, up to 6 cm long, may be rounded or egg-shaped, with yellow, red or purple skins. The flesh separates easily from the flattened stone inside, and may be sharp or sweet.

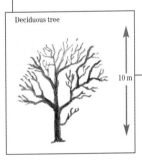

Deciduous tree

10 m

The Plum is not often seen as a truly wild tree in western Europe – it is thought to be native to the Caucasus region. It is also clearly related to the Bullace (*Prunus insititia*), which is thought to be native, and has smaller, rounder fruit with a round stone that does not separate easily from the flesh. The fruits of wild bullace are not really edible, being too sharp and disinclined to soften, though cultivated varieties include the damson and the greengage. Plums, on the other hand, are most often escapees of cultivated trees and very much worth eating, and may be found from time to time along roadsides or on sites formerly inhabited by humans.

COOKING AND EATING The fruits are usually ripe from October onwards, but there is no way of knowing whether they will be sharp or sweet until tasted. They may, of course, be used in exactly the same way as shop-bought varieties. Referring to the jam recipe on page 19, use an equal weight of stoned fruit and sugar, but if the plums are firm, then add a little water to help them soften. Very ripe plums will have less pectin than usual, so use special jam-making sugar. Or, crack some kernels, put them in a muslin bag, and place it in the jam just before the setting point is reached.

Plum forms a rounded or spreading, deciduous tree, up to 10 m high. It is most likely to be seen close to gardens or human habitation.

BARK
Grey-brown, smooth when young, but scaly and forming fissures with age.

73

Elderflower

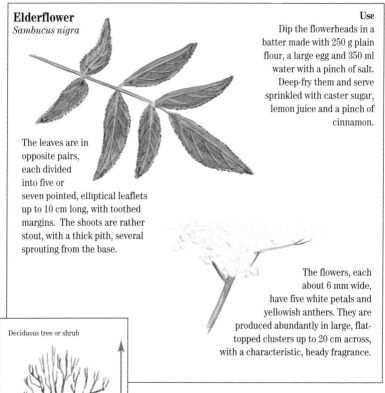

Elderflower
Sambucus nigra

Use
Dip the flowerheads in a batter made with 250 g plain flour, a large egg and 350 ml water with a pinch of salt. Deep-fry them and serve sprinkled with caster sugar, lemon juice and a pinch of cinnamon.

The leaves are in opposite pairs, each divided into five or seven pointed, elliptical leaflets up to 10 cm long, with toothed margins. The shoots are rather stout, with a thick pith, several sprouting from the base.

The flowers, each about 6 mm wide, have five white petals and yellowish anthers. They are produced abundantly in large, flat-topped clusters up to 20 cm across, with a characteristic, heady fragrance.

Deciduous tree or shrub

4-8 m

The Elder occurs twice in this book, because it offers two opportunities to sample its delights in completely different ways: once for the flowers in summer, and then again for the fruits in autumn (see page 170).

It is particularly abundant in hedgerows, woodland margins and close to old buildings. The flowers have a sweet, heady scent when freshly opened in the morning, but after a few hours of sunshine give off a slightly unpleasant, musty odour, so should be gathered before then. They can be used to flavour cordials, syrups, wines, chutneys and vinegars.

COOKING AND EATING This recipe for Elderflower syrup captures the essence of its short flowering period. Gather about 20 freshly opened flowerheads, including stalks. Dissolve 700 g of granulated sugar in 600ml of water in a large pan, heating it slowly until all the sugar has dissolved. Bring up to a rapid boil and immerse the flowerheads, pushing them down into the liquid. Remove from the heat, cover, and allow to cool. Add the juice of a lemon, then gently strain the syrup through a muslin-lined sieve, twice. The syrup is now ready for bottling, and will keep in the fridge for up to six months. Dilute with sparkling water and add a slice of lemon for a refreshing summer cordial.

Elder grows as a small tree or, more commonly, as a large shrub, and is often rather straggling, with arching stems. It is covered with numerous plate-like flowerheads in early summer. It grows throughout Europe except northern Scandinavia, and flowers in June and July.

BARK
Grey-brown, with deep furrows and a corky texture. Often colonised by Jew's Ear fungus (page 216).

Marsh Samphire

Marsh Samphire
Salicornia europaea

The leaves resemble tiny scales, fused across the stems, so that the whole plant looks like bunches of erect, fleshy fingers. The stems themselves are semi-translucent, blue- or grass-green, but often flushed with red or even entirely red, especially late in the season.

Use

For a delicious summer lunch, blanch some young Samphire shoots in boiling water, then toss them in melted butter and garlic. Serve with cooked, unshelled prawns and a large glass of strong beer or stout.

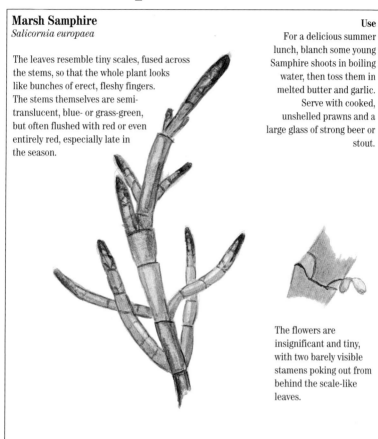

The flowers are insignificant and tiny, with two barely visible stamens poking out from behind the scale-like leaves.

Marshland

Marsh Samphire is an unusual member of the goosefoot family, along with Fat Hen (page 220) and Good King Henry (page 30), but which has almost no leaves at all; just fat, succulent stems. These are adapted to retain plenty of fresh moisture in the cells, for twice a day the plant is often covered by sea water, to no ill effect. Collecting Samphire can be a romantic, memorable, but messy business, as you often have to walk out on to mud flats at low tide. Wear rubber boots and be ready for everything to be coated with a fine silt that dries like plaster. Try to collect the bushiest specimens nearest to the high tide line, snipping off the young shoots with scissors or a knife, and leaving the muddy roots intact.

COOKING AND EATING Samphire has a tangy, salty flavour and only requires thorough washing and brief boiling before being eaten like asparagus. There tends to be a woody core to the larger branches, in which case strip away the flesh with the teeth, in much the same way as you would the leaves of a Globe Artichoke. Small shoots are excellent if served in a sauce over fish. Boil 60 ml of white wine for 2 minutes, then whisk in 60 g unsalted butter, add a handful of blanched Samphire and a few capers.

Marsh Samphire *forms huge, ankle-high carpets across salt marshes and mudflats, below the tideline, sometimes stretching for miles. There are several similar species, but they are very difficult to separate and all are edible. In warm climates, the plant may grow tall and bushy.*

Marsh Samphire

RANGE: Coasts throughout Europe, though rarer in Scandinavia.

HABITAT: Salt marshes and mudflats.

FLOWERING TIME: August to September.

Rock Samphire

Rock Samphire
Crithmum maritimum

The leaves are fleshy protuberances, flattish or cylindrical in cross-section with one or two branches pointing skywards. They are grey green, though sometimes tinged with red, and smell of polish.

The flowers, just 2 mm across, are creamy or yellowish green, clustered into rounded umbels 3-6 cm across.

Use
Strip any tough or slimy parts away. Put a handful in boiling water for about ten minutes. Serve with melted butter and black pepper and eat on the beach, sucking away the soft flesh from any stringy veins.

Coast

Rock Samphire is unrelated to the Marsh Samphire of the mudflats, in fact it is a member of the carrot family along with Cow Parsley and Fennel. It shares the name samphire partly because of the similarity of the succulent, fleshy leaves, and partly because the name samphire come from St. Pierre – the patron saint of fishermen. The leaves are adapted to conserving moisture in harsh coastal environments and have a curious resinous or sulphurous fragrance, something like polish. Rock Samphire was very popular in the 16th Century when strong flavours and robust sauces were in vogue to accompany meat. Some of the unusual aroma remains after cooking, though it largely disappears on pickling, which used to be the fate of most Rock Samphires – it was once quite an industry.

COOKING AND EATING Gather the young leaves in June or July before the plant has flowered, soak in water for 1 hour, then cook in boiling water for ten minutes. In a separate pan, boil together for 5 minutes 3 cups of white pickling vinegar with 1 cup water, 1 tsp salt, 3 tsp pickling spices, peppercorns and dried mace. Bottle the Rock Samphire with the vinegar mixture and leave for four months to allow it to mellow.

Rock Samphire *is a bushy, clump-forming plant growing to about knee-high on coastal rocks, cliffs, sand or shingle. It appears when summer is well underway, eventually producing tight umbels of creamy yellow flowers. It is best to gather the plant before flowering in order to get the tenderest shoots.*

Rock Samphire

RANGE: Atlantic and Mediterranean coasts of Europe, southern and western coasts of British Isles.

HABITAT: Costal rocks, cliffs, sand or shingle.

FLOWERING TIME: August to September.

Sea Kale

Sea Kale
Crambe maritima

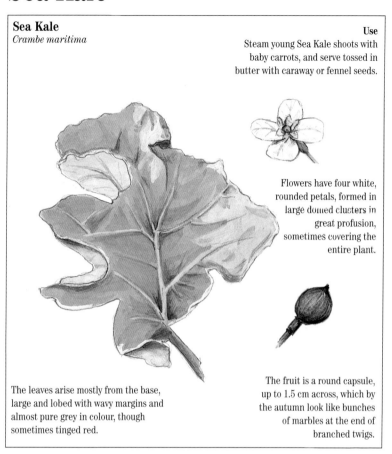

Flowers have four white, rounded petals, formed in large domed clusters in great profusion, sometimes covering the entire plant.

The leaves arise mostly from the base, large and lobed with wavy margins and almost pure grey in colour, though sometimes tinged red.

The fruit is a round capsule, up to 1.5 cm across, which by the autumn look like bunches of marbles at the end of branched twigs.

Coast

The great clumps of grey-green, waxy leaves of Sea Kale are difficult to miss in the barren landscape of a shingle beach or coastal sands. They are succulent, lobed, and with wavy margins, like those of a cabbage. The young leaves are furled, with crisped edges, and often tinged red. It is these younger leaves that are usually eaten: but their robust texture means that even they tend to be tough. For this reason, they were often blanched before being picked, either by placing pots over them, or simply piling up the shingle over the youngest shoots. This made the leaves tall, pale and tender. Unfortunately, the method was so effective, and popular, that Sea Kale suffered a dramatic decline; it is now far less common than it was. So, it is best to pick a few young shoots, leaving the rest of the plant untouched.

COOKING AND EATING They may be cooked like cabbage, or fried and steamed as in this recipe: melt 30 g of butter in a large pan and continue to heat gently until it starts to turn brown. Add some Sea Kale leaves, stripped from the midrib and chopped, with finely chopped garlic and chopped hazel nuts or walnuts, and the juice and zest of half a lemon. Toss the leaves and nuts in the butter and continue cooking until tender.

***Sea Kale** forms large clumps or mounds up to knee height, often close to the shoreline, on shingle beaches, sandy beaches, cliffs and sea walls. Even when the plant is not covered in white flowers, the thick, waxy grey leaves make it instantly recognisable.*

Sea Kale

RANGE: Coasts of Britain, Ireland, France and Scandinavia.

HABITAT: Coast.

FLOWERING TIME: June to August.

Meadowsweet

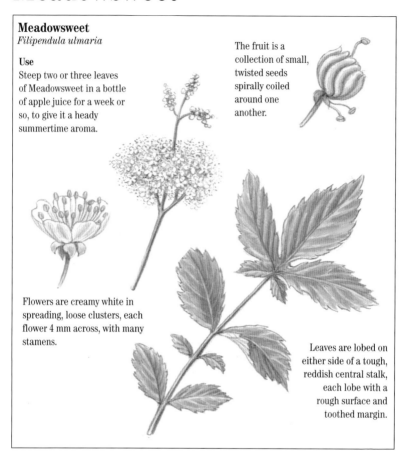

Meadowsweet
Filipendula ulmaria

Use
Steep two or three leaves of Meadowsweet in a bottle of apple juice for a week or so, to give it a heady summertime aroma.

The fruit is a collection of small, twisted seeds spirally coiled around one another.

Flowers are creamy white in spreading, loose clusters, each flower 4 mm across, with many stamens.

Leaves are lobed on either side of a tough, reddish central stalk, each lobe with a rough surface and toothed margin.

Marshland

Meadowsweet is a delightful herb that produces graceful, delicate tufts of creamy-white blooms throughout the summer. The loose, frothy sprays of flowers may at first sight be taken as those of a member of the carrot family, but this plant is actually related to the rose. The leaves produce a cucumber scent, but the flowers have the heady, almost sickly fragrance of honey and almonds, and were used for 'strewing' the floors of 16th-Century homes to impart a sweet scent and drive away insects. The little, round buds contain salicylic acid and were first used for synthesizing aspirin: a tea made from the flowers makes an excellent mild painkiller. The leaves have been shown to reduce the ulcers sometimes caused by pure aspirin.

COOKING AND EATING The flowers are still sometimes used for flavouring beer, and the dried leaves were used to season honey wine, or mead. The leaves contain a high proportion of coumarin, the substance that gives its fragrance to new-mown hay. For a fresh, summer punch, steep a few dried leaves in a bottle of medium white wine for a day or two. Mix it with an equal quantity of clear apple juice and about 50g of sugar dissolved in warm water. Serve chilled with slices of cucumber and orange.

Meadowsweet often grows chest-high in the lush vegetation of marshy meadows or along a river bank, and is easily recognized by the irregularly shaped foamy clusters of flowers, like candy-floss on a stick. It often grows in great masses and stands high above other vegetation.

Meadowsweet

RANGE: Throughout Europe.

HABITAT: Damp grassland, riversides.

FLOWERING TIME: June to September.

Common Poppy

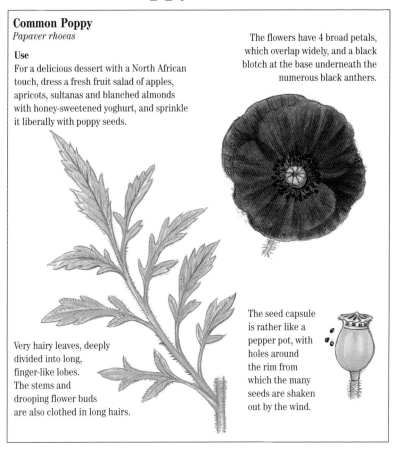

Common Poppy
Papaver rhoeas

Use
For a delicious dessert with a North African touch, dress a fresh fruit salad of apples, apricots, sultanas and blanched almonds with honey-sweetened yoghurt, and sprinkle it liberally with poppy seeds.

The flowers have 4 broad petals, which overlap widely, and a black blotch at the base underneath the numerous black anthers.

Very hairy leaves, deeply divided into long, finger-like lobes. The stems and drooping flower buds are also clothed in long hairs.

The seed capsule is rather like a pepper pot, with holes around the rim from which the many seeds are shaken out by the wind.

Farmland

The seeds of the Common Poppy may lie dormant in the ground for many years, but when they are brought to the surface, perhaps when a field has been ploughed more deeply than usual or after a period of neglect, then poppy flowers may be very abundant, seemingly outnumbering the crop that has been planted there. The tiny black seeds are used to decorate and add flavour to bread, though there is little truth in the theory that they help to induce sleep in children, since this plant contains none of the morphine, narcotine and codeine found in the juice of the related Opium Poppy (*Papaver somniferum*), which usually has larger, pink or white flowers.

COOKING AND EATING Collect the seeds by gathering a few of the ripe capsules in a paper bag and hanging them upside down in a dry place until all the seeds have fallen out into the bag. Mixed with herbs, they are ideal for flavouring dumplings to serve with a beef stew. They also add a delicious piquancy to spring vegetables. Very gently sautée thinly sliced carrots in a covered pan with a knob of butter for 10 minutes. Add enough water to cover them, bring to the boil and add a robust green vegetable, such as sea spinach, Good King Henry, broccoli or kale. Sprinkle with poppy seeds just before serving.

Common Poppy *forms a brilliant scarlet carpet in fields and cannot possibly be confused with anything else. Whole fields may be coloured bright red and they may be seen from a great distance. Not surprisingly, poppies have been an inspiration for impressionist artists such as Claude Monet.*

Common Poppy

RANGE: Throughout Europe, except the extreme north and much of Finland.

HABITAT: Farmland.

FLOWERING TIME: June to September.

Horseradish

Horseradish

Armoracia rusticana

Use

A warm horseradish sauce for pouring can be made by adding 1 teaspoon of grated Horseradish to a hot white sauce made with butter, flour and milk. The heat drives off some of the volatile oils, so it is milder than the cold horseradish cream below.

Flowers are only occasionally formed, when the leaves are still rather small and easily taken for those of dock. They occur in broad clusters on narrow-leaved stems up to 1 m high; each flower is about 1 cm wide with 4 white oval petals. The fruit – a rounded inflated pod about 8 mm across – is rarely formed.

The leaves are large and stout, usually bolt-upright on long stalks. They are a little like the leaves of dock, but develop characteristically wavy margins, with a crinkled leaf surface and a pale midrib. They smell faintly of Horseradish if crushed. In late summer, sets of narrowly lobed leaves sometimes appear.

As the season progresses, the roots develop. They are carrot-like, white and fleshy, up to 5 cm thick and 50 cm long.

Wasteland

Horseradish is a native of southern Russia, but it has been cultivated throughout Europe since the Middle Ages. It occurs quite commonly on wasteground and field margins, or even in scraps of soil next to buildings, wherever the earth is disturbed. The plant is related to those whose seeds are used to make mustard, but in this instance the mustard oil is concentrated in the root, so it must be dug up, or partly dug up, to obtain the edible part. The plant easily regrows from even small sections of root left in the soil, so with care it should not be destroyed by the operation, which can take place until early winter.

COOKING AND EATING Take care when preparing the vegetable as the volatile oils are extremely strong; it may be a good idea to wear gloves when handling it. To make horseradish cream, mix together 150 ml double cream, 1 tablespoon white vinegar, 1 teaspoon English mustard and 1 teaspoon caster sugar. Gradually mix in 2 tablespoons of very finely grated Horseradish, tasting along the way until the desired strength is achieved. Finally, season with salt and pepper. The cream will keep in the fridge for up to a month. Serve with roast beef or smoked oily fish such as mackerel.

Horseradish *appears as tufts of upright, wavy leaves at about knee height; they last throughout the summer and are easily identified by their smell. The flowers, which reach to waist height, may not be produced at all in some years, although they are more common in warmer climates.*

Horseradish

RANGE: Throughout Europe, except northern Britain and northern Scandinavia.

HABITAT: Waste ground and field margins.

FLOWERING TIME: May to July.

Salad Burnet

Salad Burnet
Sanguisorba minor

Use

Infuse a few bruised Salad Burnet leaves in a jug of medium white wine for a couple of hours, then sweeten to taste and dilute with soda water for a cooling summer punch.

The leaves have small opposite lobes spaced out along the mid-rib, each toothed so they look like little bird's wings.

Flowers are in a spherical head about 2 cm across, greenish with crimson styles protruding, later followed by drooping male anthers.

Delicately divided, lacy leaves, with small bluntly-toothed lobes on long curved stalks.

Grassy meadows

It may be difficult to guess that this is a member of the rose family, for the flowers are not immediately obvious, like little pom-poms on a short stalk. There are no petals as such, but when the bright red female styles burst out then whole areas of the landscape may be coloured by them, as the plant grows in profusion among dry grassland and rocky places on chalky soils. The styles are closely followed by the male yellow anthers which droop down on thin filaments. *Sanguisorba* (absorber of blood) gets its name from the fact that, like its relative the Great Burnet (*Sanguisorba officinalis*), the leaves have styptic and astringent properties. The leaves have the faint scent of cucumber, but something of a bitter taste. The plant was held in great esteem in the past as a tonic, and imbued with remarkable properties of staving off the plague, or pestilence, and to 'defend the heart from noysome vapours'. Sadly none of these claims are true, but it makes a welcome addition to salads, provided that young leaves are used, and in limited quantity.

COOKING AND EATING Try a simple salad using Chickweed or Ground Elder as a base, topped with ripe, sliced tomatoes mixed with a few leaves of Salad Burnet. Crumble some blue cheese over, such as Cambozola, and finish with a dressing of extra virgin olive oil.

Salad Burnet *grows usually little more than ankle-high, and may go unnoticed except for when the crimson styles open out on the flower-heads like little red lollipops. The leaves persist for some months after flowering, but use the youngest for salads.*

Salad Burnet

RANGE: Throughout Europe except northern
Scandinavia and Scotland.

HABITAT: Dry grassland and rocky soils.

FLOWERING TIME: May to July.

Raspberry

Raspberry
Rubus idaeus

Use
Try making uncooked raspberry jam by pre-warming some caster sugar in a low oven, then mixing and mashing it with the same weight of Raspberries until the sugar has dissolved. Seal into sterilized jars and keep in the fridge for up to a month, or in the freezer for much longer.

The flowers, 10 mm wide, are understated and difficult to spot, nodding in clusters. They have five, small white petals, much smaller than the triangular green sepals that separate them. In the centre there is a cluster of stamens resembling a little brush.

The leaves are divided into 5 or 7 pointed, oval lobes with serrated margins. They are pale green above, but with whitish down beneath. They are on arching stems with weak, often recurved prickles, much less fierce than those of Blackberry.

The fruit is a slightly elongated cluster of bright orange-red, slightly hairy drupelets, easily pulled away from the sepal when ripe to leave behind a small, cone-shaped structure.

Woodland

Raspberries are not uncommon in the wild, but are easily overlooked because the untidy bushes they form may be dismissed as those of Blackberry. The flowers are far less showy, and the fruit generally produced in smaller quantities. It occurs in shady areas in woodland and scrub, or on heaths, wasteland and embankments. The berries are dispersed by birds, but many apparantly wild plants may be the result of discarded fruit from someone's picnic. The fruit is not necessarily any less sweet than that of cultivated varieties, but may be more orange-red than crimson. If you find a useful number, collect them to make a raspberry *coulis*.

COOKING AND EATING Blend 200 g Raspberries with 50 g of icing sugar, or more if the Raspberries are especially acid. The *coulis* can be used as a sauce for a variety of desserts such as an ice cream sundae, or to decorate pastries. Or use the *coulis* for an Eton Mess: crush some *Cantucci* biscuits (or other honey-and-almond biscuits) so they resemble breadcrumbs. Mix together with 2 tbsp Greek yoghurt, 2 tbsp double cream, 100g mascarpone cream cheese and 50g blanched almonds. Layer the mixture in a tall glass with swirls of raspberry coulis, and decorate with a leaf of Lemon Balm.

Raspberry *is a waist- to chest-high suckering perennial, with long, arching non-branching stems. It is rather more delicate than the closely-related Blackberry, and more likely to be found in sheltered or shady situations.*

Raspberry

RANGE: Throughout Europe, except for Portugal, western France and Italy.

HABITAT: Woodlands, scrub, heaths, wasteland and embankments.

FLOWERING TIME: May to August.

Wild Strawberry

Wild Strawberry
Fragaria vesca

Use
The leaves have a long history of medicinal uses, particularly for digestive disorders.

The flowers, each 12-18 mm across, have 5 rounded white petals that just touch each other, with the sepals peeping out between them, and a cluster of yellow anthers in the centre.

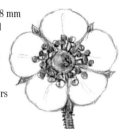

The fruit is a small, delicious strawberry, ripening from green to red. The seeds are held in tiny pits on the fruit's surface.

Each long-stalked leaf is divided into three toothed leaflets. Barren Strawberry (*Potentilla sterilis*) is similar, but the end tooth on each leaflet is smaller, and the flower petals do not overlap.

Woodland

Wild Strawberry is easily overlooked, since the small, rose-like flowers often only just peep out from between the long-stalked leaves. The fruits are tiny, but have a sweet, delicate flavour, even finer than the cultivated varieties with much larger fruits that sometimes escape into the wild. They are difficult to find, so search underneath the leaves, which will have grown quite large by midsummer. Fruits gathered from warm, sheltered spots will have the best flavour.

COOKING AND EATING Recipes that make use of the fruits' flavour, rather than quantity, are best. One such is to make a jelly from diluted elderflower cordial (page 74) and gelatine. Pour it into champagne or cocktail glasses and add a few wild strawberries. The fruits will float, so pour the molten jelly in two or three layers, adding some fruit each time, and allow it to set slightly in the fridge between pourings. Beat the remaining jelly with a whisk until it is frothy and spoon it over the top – when set, it will look just like champagne.

Wild Strawberries may be preserved by mashing them with a little sugar, then spreading the paste very thinly on a baking sheet. Dry it in a low oven (100°C) until it is crisp, and add pieces to breakfast cereal.

Wild Strawberry *is a secretive plant, hugging the ground and sometimes hiding its attractive flowers among the three-lobed and strongly toothed, deeply veined leaves, which are in many ways its most distinctive feature. Often there are flowers and ripe fruit on the plant at the same time.*

Wild Strawberry

RANGE: Throughout Europe.

HABITAT: Sunny light woodland, railway banks, heaths, rocky outcrops, old walls.

FLOWERING TIME Flowers, April to July. Fruit, May to August.

93

Gooseberry

Gooseberry
Ribes uva-crispum

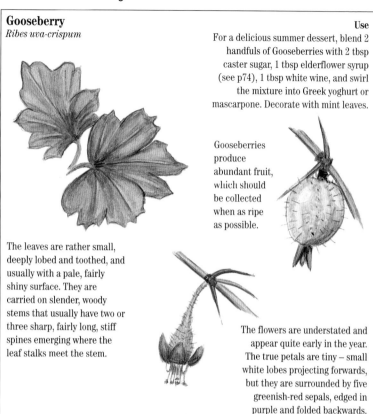

Use
For a delicious summer dessert, blend 2 handfuls of Gooseberries with 2 tbsp caster sugar, 1 tbsp elderflower syrup (see p74), 1 tbsp white wine, and swirl the mixture into Greek yoghurt or mascarpone. Decorate with mint leaves.

Gooseberries produce abundant fruit, which should be collected when as ripe as possible.

The leaves are rather small, deeply lobed and toothed, and usually with a pale, fairly shiny surface. They are carried on slender, woody stems that usually have two or three sharp, fairly long, stiff spines emerging where the leaf stalks meet the stem.

The flowers are understated and appear quite early in the year. The true petals are tiny – small white lobes projecting forwards, but they are surrounded by five greenish-red sepals, edged in purple and folded backwards.

Hedgerows, scrub

Like the Raspberry, Gooseberry is another scrubby, tangled plant that may easily be passed by without a second look, though once you know them the leaves are distinctive enough. It is native to parts of Europe, but has been so extensively cultivated that it now occurs almost everywhere, and most wild plants are probably the result of past escapes from gardens. It occurs in sheltered spots in hedgerows, scrub, woodland clearings or close to buildings. Blackcurrant and Redcurrant are two very similar, though spineless, species, and can be easily identified only when the fruit has formed, though few berries are produced in the wild. Gooseberry, however, frequently forms abundant fruit: collect them with some caution to avoid the spines. Try to find those that are as ripe as possible and will therefore contain the most sugar. They always need to be 'topped and tailed' with a sharp knife to remove the stalk and persistent sepals.

COOKING AND EATING This tangy sauce goes very well with slow-roasted pork or mackerel: very gently stew 250 g of Gooseberries with a little butter in 150ml water or cider. Mash them, and rub the pulp through a sieve. Reheat the juice and stir in 25g of sugar, half a tsp mustard, salt, pepper and nutmeg, and some finely chopped leaves of either Sorrel, Wood Sorrel, Hairy Bittercress or Fennel.

Gooseberry *forms a branched and spiny shrub growing to chest height, often in a tangled thicket by a hedgerow. Easy to miss, the tiny flowers usually go unseen, and it takes a sharp eye to spot the hairy green berries hanging in ones and twos among the leaves in June or July.*

Gooseberry

RANGE: Throughout Europe except for Portugal and south-western Spain, and the far North.

HABITAT: Hedgerows, scrub and woodlands.

FLOWERING TIME: March to May.

Common Mallow

Common Mallow
Malva sylvestris

Use
For a nibble to go with drinks, gather the small nutlets before they are ripe and hard, and roast them briefly in a pan with a little butter, salt and paprika.

Leaves are more or less kidney shaped, wavy or wrinkled, and with shallow teeth on the margin.

The flowers have 5 well-separated deep pink petals, each with a distinct notch and radiating lines of mauve or magenta.

Rough wasteland

The disturbed soils of wasteground, abandoned fields and the edges of cultivation are the habitat of Common Mallow. Its cheerful pink flowers appear in midsummer, and it goes on to produce them for several months, but as it does so, the soft leaves inevitably become eaten by insects and snails, and the whole plant takes on a dishevelled and straggly appearance. The fruits are produced as a ring of nutlets joined together like the segments of an orange, but have also been likened to a miniature cheese.

COOKING AND EATING The leaves of Common Mallow have a high content of mucilage, a quality that makes them invaluable not only as a poultice for bruises but also as a thickener for stews and soups. One such, Melokhia, is an important traditional dish of Egypt. It is something of an acquired taste, but the secret of it is to use a really good flavoursome stock. Finely chop 500 g young, well-washed Mallow leaves and sautée them in butter until soft. Add 1 litre hot chicken or vegetable stock and simmer for 5 minutes. Meanwhile, fry in olive oil a paste of crushed garlic, ground coriander seeds and cayenne or paprika, to taste. Mix the paste into the soup, adding some fresh Coriander leaves. Serve by pouring over boiled rice and decorate with a Mallow flower.

Common Mallow *is often an untidy and scruffy plant of waist-height or thereabouts, but with neat flowers that look as though they have been crafted in porcelain. In some areas, and particularly close to the sea, it may grow as a sprawling, prostrate plant.*

Common Mallow

RANGE: Throughout Europe, except much of Scandinavia.

HABITAT: Rough wasteland, abandoned fields.

FLOWERING TIME: June to September.

Chicory

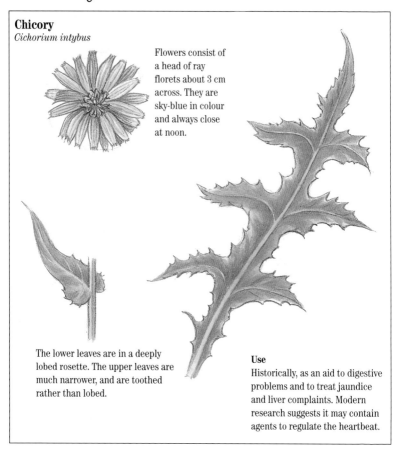

Chicory
Cichorium intybus

Flowers consist of a head of ray florets about 3 cm across. They are sky-blue in colour and always close at noon.

The lower leaves are in a deeply lobed rosette. The upper leaves are much narrower, and are toothed rather than lobed.

Use
Historically, as an aid to digestive problems and to treat jaundice and liver complaints. Modern research suggests it may contain agents to regulate the heartbeat.

Hedgerows, roadsides

Chicory flowers are the most extraordinary sky-blue: especially remarkable as it is a member of the daisy family, allied to Dandelions, the flowers of which are commonly yellow or white. It grows on grassy embankments and roadsides, waste places and rough fields, usually among tall grasses on chalky soil, but is easily passed by unless seen in the morning, since the brightly coloured flowers close at midday. It is sometimes grown in gardens, particularly in one of its pink forms, but cultivated varieties are always inferior to the splendour of the natural plant.

COOKING AND EATING The leaves are bitter, but are nonetheless a delicious ingredient in salads – the winter leaves are less bitter than the summer ones – or it can be used as a winter vegetable if the young leaves are blanched, either by removing the lower ones and piling up earth around the stem, or by placing a pot over the plant to exclude the light. This reduces the bitterness to a palatable level. The roots, like those of Dandelion, are also bitter, and they may be cooked like parsnip; they add a rich colour if used in soups and stews. Dried, roasted and ground they make a caffeine-free substitute for coffee; more usually though, the powder is added to real coffee for the particular flavour it imparts.

Chicory's tall, almost leafless spires reach up to chest-height, sporting their pale blue flowers above the long grass. They are an unusual colour for a flower that is a member of the daisy family, whose members usually have yellow or white flowers.

Chicory

RANGE: Throughout Europe,
except northern Scandinavia and much of Ireland.

HABITAT: Roadsides, waste places, rough fields.

FLOWERING TIME: July to October.

Wild Asparagus

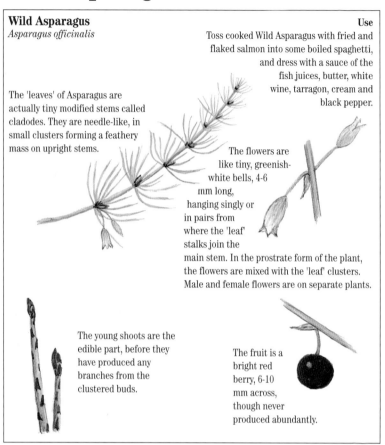

Wild Asparagus
Asparagus officinalis

The 'leaves' of Asparagus are actually tiny modified stems called cladodes. They are needle-like, in small clusters forming a feathery mass on upright stems.

Use
Toss cooked Wild Asparagus with fried and flaked salmon into some boiled spaghetti, and dress with a sauce of the fish juices, butter, white wine, tarragon, cream and black pepper.

The flowers are like tiny, greenish-white bells, 4-6 mm long, hanging singly or in pairs from where the 'leaf' stalks join the main stem. In the prostrate form of the plant, the flowers are mixed with the 'leaf' clusters. Male and female flowers are on separate plants.

The young shoots are the edible part, before they have produced any branches from the clustered buds.

The fruit is a bright red berry, 6-10 mm across, though never produced abundantly.

Grassy meadows

Wild Asparagus is a rather unusual member of the lily family without any true leaves. Instead, the stems are highly branched into numerous clustered portions, resembling pine needles, so that the whole plant has a feathery appearance. It is difficult to predict exactly where Wild Asparagus will occur, as it is rather local in distribution, but it can be found in scrub, or in grassy places, woodland clearings, or on cultivated or disturbed soils. It is frequent in eastern and south-eastern Europe, and has been cultivated elsewhere for thousands of years. Only the young shoots are edible, when just a few centimetres high. They look like cultivated Asparagus spears, except they are much slimmer, and never blanched white. It is difficult to find the spears growing among grass or other vegetation, so the best technique is to look for fronds that have fully emerged and examine the base of the plant for further shoots. As the plant is perennial, it may be visited in the same location the following year, but early enough to catch the first green spears. Cut just a few, leaving the rest of the plant intact.

COOKING AND EATING Boil the spears for just a few minutes until tender, and dress simply with butter and black pepper.

Wild Asparagus *grows to waist height when fully formed, with a feathery, fern-like appearance, never growing in large clumps or colonies. The flowers are too small and colourless to be noticeable. Look for the shoots as early as possible in the year.*

Wild Asparagus

RANGE: Throughout most of Europe, except for northern Scandinavia and northern Britain.

HABITAT: Scrubby grassland.

FLOWERING TIME: June to August.

Coriander

Coriander
Coriandrum sativum

The seeds should only be used when fully ripe and brown. Their flavour complements pork, lamb and even fish. Try adding some to the pan when frying sausages to give them a warm, spicy flavour.

The small flowers (3-5 mm across) are white or pink-tinged, growing in umbels of three to five rays. About 15 tiny flowers are clustered at the end of each ray, but the outer petals of some of them are considerably enlarged and divided into two. There are no drooping bracts below the flowers as in Fool's Parsley (*Aethusa cynapium*), which is poisonous.

The upper leaves are divided two or three times into narrow, almost linear segments, so they have a feathery and insubstantial appearance. The lower leaves are different, divided into three or five broad lobes, each leaflet in turn irregularly lobed and toothed. Only the lower leaves are used as a herb.

The fruit is a rounded capsule, 3-6 mm in diameter, with fine surface ridges. It is pale brown when ripe. They remain in very tight, stalkless clusters on the umbel rays. Seeds of wild plants are usually no bigger than 3 mm.

Wasteland

This small, innocuous-looking plant is thought to originate from the eastern Mediterranean and northern Africa, but is now naturalized in many places throughout Europe. The seeds have long been held in great esteem, with a warm, nutty and spicy aroma, and are sometimes said to have a hint of orange or lemon. They are a traditional ingredient of curries and north African or Asian dishes. There is, however, much disagreement about the use of the leaves as a herb, especially in Europe and North America where it is known as *cilantro*. Some say it smells foetid, soapy, rubbery or like squashed bedbugs. Others find it completely delicious. The following recipe for spicy butternut squash soup should convince the most hardened sceptic.

COOKING AND EATING Remove the skin and seeds from an average-sized squash, and add the chopped flesh to a saucepan with chopped onion, garlic, and one small chilli pepper. Add 500 ml of vegetable stock and simmer until the squash is soft. Liquidise in a blender, and add half a can of coconut milk. Add water (if necessary – water comes out of the squash), and season. Simmer, then add half a cup of fresh Coriander leaves. A few cooked prawns added at this stage will make the soup even better.

Coriander *is a short, weedy-looking plant between ankle- and knee-height, growing in waste or bare places and easily dismissed until recognised. The two forms of leaf however are distinctive, as are the tiny umbels of flowers with eccentric petals. If in doubt, look for the almost spherical fruits, and smell the leaves.*

Coriander

RANGE: Central and eastern France and Germany, casual elsewhere, including Britain.

HABITAT: Waste or bare areas.

FLOWERING TIME: June to August.

Sweet Cicely

Sweet Cicely
Myrrhis odorata

Use

Infuse a few Sweet Cicely leaves in 2 tbsp white wine over a moderate heat for 5 minutes. Strain, and whip together with 2 tbsp sugar and 280 ml of double cream for the perfect topping to stewed fruit.

The tiny, pure white flowers are in large umbels of up to 20 rays, without any leaf-like bracts beneath them.

Fern-like leaves, triangular in outline and divided into numerous lacey lobes, and with a sheath-like wing curving up on each side at the base of the leaf stalk. The stems are green, without any red spots.

The fruits are very characteristic, the largest of any umbellifer, up to 25 mm long, with longitudinal ridges. Green at first, eventually ripening dark brown.

Roadsides, meadows

Sweet Cicely, though superficially similar to Cow Parsley (page 42), has a neater, more refined appearance. It is common only in the cooler, shadier parts of upland regions, and often found growing near water. It is immediately identifiable by the scent of its leaves, which have a light aniseed fragrance. They also taste as though they have been dusted with sugar: this plant is sweet throughout. However, always look for the uniquely large upright fruits before tasting – you need to avoid any confusion with the deadly Hemlock. The leaves may be used (like those of Fennel) in fish dishes, and have a flavour somewhere between Celery and Aniseed. They go superbly with vegetables such as carrots, sprouts or cabbage if a handful of chopped leaves are added to the pot when cooking. The seeds have been likened to those of Caraway, but they have a finer, sweeter flavour and may be used in breads and cakes, as well as with meatballs or fishcakes. They are at their best when still green and soft.

COOKING AND EATING Roughly chop some cooking apples and gently stew them for 15 minutes or so with sugar to taste, adding a tsp of chopped, green Sweet Cicely seeds. Use the puree as a delicious sauce for roast pork.

Sweet Cicely grows to chest height, forming cloud-like billows of ferny leaves along roadsides and meadows, chiefly in upland or mountainous areas. It has a pale, fresh green colour, topped with flat clusters of snow-white flowers, followed by upright fruits, like tiny miniature gherkins.

Sweet Cicely

RANGE: Upland regions of most of Europe, and mountain ranges further south.

HABITAT: Upland regions, often near water.

FLOWERING TIME: May to July.

Heather

Heather
Calluna vulgaris

Use
Dress roasted game, such as pheasant, grouse or venison, with flowering tops of Heather just before serving. The warmth from the meat will release a delicious sweet aroma from the flowers.

The leaves are like tiny scales in opposite pairs. They overlap one another, almost like the shoots of a moss.

The flowers are just 3 mm long, drooping from densely-packed, long conical spires. Pink, pale purple, lilac and occasionally white forms are produced.

Heathland

Heather is a familiar plant of dry sandy soils, which also grows as a straggly plant in the clearings and rides of open woodland. But it is better known as the staple inhabitant of wide-open heathlands and moors, which were created by man through the clearance of trees to provide low-grade grazing pasture. The plant was an invaluable resource for peasant communities: its springy, woody branches were used to stuff mattresses; to thatch roofs; to strengthen primitive mud-and-clay walls; and it was made into household articles such as brooms and rope. The abundance of the flowers and the sweetness of their nectar make it a favourite of beekeepers, and the flowering tops have been used for making beer, a practice recently revived on a commercial scale in Scotland. The young shoots are surprisingly soft and palatable, and provide food for game birds such as grouse.

COOKING AND EATING Heather makes a very palatable and rather impressive after-dinner tea, especially if served in a transparent glass teapot or cafetiere. Infuse a few fresh flowering tops in just-boiled water, adding a leaf or two of Balm to give a lemony note. Sweeten with a little honey, which should, of course, be heather honey.

106

Heather forms springy clumps from ankle- to waist-height, which are straggly and woody at the base. It is often in huge colonies, colouring the landscape when in flower. Although it grows slowly, it lives a long time. The tiny leaves, in pairs on small branches, are leathery, becoming rough to the touch as they mature.

Heather

RANGE: Throughout Europe.

HABITAT: Heathland. open woodland.

FLOWERING TIME: July to September.

107

Bilberry

Bilberry
Vaccinium myrtillus

Use
For a Christmas tipple, make Bilberry brandy by mashing 500 g Bilberries with 100 g sugar. Add a bottle of brandy, and keep in a closed jar for at least 3 months, stirring regularly. Strain before use.

The flowers are tiny (5 mm) pendent red or green bells hanging from the stiff, ribbed stems.

The simple, oval-shaped leaves are rather small and delicate, with a slightly toothed margin. As the season progresses, they change colour from a rosy red to yellow-green and back to red again.

The fruits, 6 mm across, are round but flattened at one end, blue-black and covered with a whitish bloom.

Heathland

This diminutive shrub prefers acid soils, and it may cover large areas of heaths and moors, particularly in the north and west, or on mountains. It also occurs under the light shade of pine woods. The fruits of the Bilberry are delicious, but their small size and haphazard distribution on the plant makes collecting them laborious: it must be done by hand, even if the berries are for commercial use. They are slightly sharp to the taste, and make excellent jam when combined with sugar, although rather a large quantity needs to be collected to make this worthwhile. The deep blue-black colour of the juice was used in the dyeing industry. The fruits ripen in August, and the slender green stems need to be lifted to reveal the little black jewels beneath.

COOKING AND EATING To make the most of just a few Bilberries, incorporate them into some fresh muffins. Mix 225 g self-raising flour with 60 g caster sugar. Separately, mix 250 ml milk, 50 g melted butter and a few drops of vanilla essence, and stir into the flour mixture. Fold in 100 g Bilberries, without squashing them, and spoon the mixture into small greased muffin tins or cases, leaving enough room for them to rise. Bake for about 20 minutes at 180–200°C, and leave to cool before turning them out.

Bilberry *may be easily dismissed as a low, knee-high shrubby plant of little interest, but it is worth looking below the leaves for the bell-like flowers or blue-black fruits. It usually grows in fairly extensive colonies, and is just as likely to be found in open pine woods as it is on the open moorland.*

Bilberry

RANGE: Throughout Europe,
but avoiding the drier lowlands of France.

HABITAT: Heathland, open pine woods.

FLOWERING TIME: April to June, fruits ripe in August.

Cranberry

Cranberry
Vaccinium oxycoccus

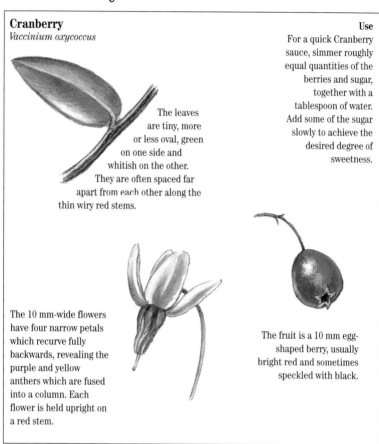

The leaves are tiny, more or less oval, green on one side and whitish on the other. They are often spaced far apart from each other along the thin wiry red stems.

Use
For a quick Cranberry sauce, simmer roughly equal quantities of the berries and sugar, together with a tablespoon of water. Add some of the sugar slowly to achieve the desired degree of sweetness.

The 10 mm-wide flowers have four narrow petals which recurve fully backwards, revealing the purple and yellow anthers which are fused into a column. Each flower is held upright on a red stem.

The fruit is a 10 mm egg-shaped berry, usually bright red and sometimes speckled with black.

Heathland

Cranberry is a member of the heather family, but an unusual one in both the form of its flowers and its growth habit. It sprawls over Sphagnum moss and other plants in wet, boggy habitats, as its thin, wiry stems – like strands of red cotton – are too weak to support its own weight. The flowers bear a resemblance to those of the unrelated Bittersweet and other members of the potato family, with strongly recurved petals and stamens fused into a projecting column. The fruit is rather acid in taste, but when preserved with sugar is said to be superior in flavour to the American plant (*Vaccinium macrocarpon*) which has larger berries, and is used in commercial preparations.

COOKING AND EATING Picking wild Cranberries is a slow business, as the fruits are never very numerous, and care must be taken not to take too many from the wild. Only a few are needed to make a rich sauce for Christmas game or poultry. To 1 cup of Cranberries add half to 1 cup of sugar, 20 g butter, a small glass of port and half a cup of water. Bring to the boil and simmer for about 10 minutes, but cover the pan as the berries can jump out when they pop. The sauce will set to a thick jelly as it cools.

Cranberry *is difficult to spot sprawling over the surface of moss, as neither the leaves nor the flowers are very numerous. The plant may sometimes be detected at a distance as a reddish haze over the ground.*

Cranberry

RANGE: Most of Europe, except the South and West.

HABITAT: Wet, boggy habitats.

FLOWERING TIME: June to July.

Cowberry

Cowberry
Vaccinium vitis-idaea

Use
Make a quick sauce for game by simmering Cowberries with an equal weight of caster sugar, a glass of red wine and a sprig of thyme. When the fruit has thoroughly softened, strain through a sieve, and serve.

Each flower is just 6-8 mm long, but there are always several clustered together. The tips of each of the four pinkish-white petals curve outwards slightly.

The oval leaves, which become wider towards the end, have a leathery appearance. They are glossy above, much paler on the underside, which is dotted with tiny black glands. There is a small notch at the very tip, and the leaf margins curve under slightly.

The fruit is an acid-tasting, egg-shaped berry, which ripens from green to yellow to brilliant scarlet.

Heathland

Cowberry is a member of the heather family, closely related to the Bilberry (page 108), but with this species the flowers are of the palest pink. The four petals are fused together into a short tube, except that the tips of each are folded back slightly so that the flowers are like a cluster of little bells. Any similarity with Bilberry ends with the fruit: those of Cowberry are bright red, with a sharp, acid taste. It forms clumps of low bushes, usually not more than 50 cm high.

COOKING AND EATING The Cowberry is closest to the Cranberry in flavour, too sharp to eat from the bush, but excellent in jellies, jams and sauces. A Cowberry and orange jelly makes a superb partner for wild duck. Using the basic jelly recipe on page 20, add the rind of 1 orange to 500 g of Cowberries, and simmer with 200 ml of orange juice in a covered pan. After the Cowberries have been strained, add 450 g of sugar to each 600 ml of juice, and boil until the setting point is reached in the usual fashion. Another alternative is to make Crabapple jelly (page 168), but substituting half of the apples with Cowberries. Add a glass of port wine to the juice before adding the sugar. This jelly goes really well with roast pork.

Cowberry *forms rounded, compact knee-high bushes which are dotted with clusters of the palest pink bells, and then later with red berries. It takes a while to collect enough of the rather sharp berries for a meal, which should be done during mid- to late autumn.*

Cowberry

RANGE: Almost throughout Europe in upland areas.

HABITAT: Moors, heaths and coniferous woods on acid soils.

FLOWERING TIME: June to August.

113

Borage

Borage
Borago officinalis

Use
Pull the freshly emerged flowers away from the hairy calyx and place one in each compartment of an ice cube tray. Fill with water to liven up ice cubes for a party.

The unmistakeable flowers are produced in nodding clusters on reddish stems, each with five bright blue, slightly recurved petals and a white centre. From this emerge the black stamens, often fused together into a little pointed cone.

The leaves are mostly near the bottom of the plant, oblong or oval, with rather wavy margins and a rough surface. The entire plant is covered in white hairs, especially prevalent on the stems, where they appear like tiny glass fibres, giving them a frosted appearance.

Wasteland

Borage is native to the Mediterranean region, but has been cultivated for centuries throughout Europe. It was thought to have remarkable medicinal properties for dealing with such conditions as 'sadness' and 'melancholy', and does indeed have mild anti-depressant constituents. The leaves have a slight cucumber taste, which is particularly brought out when added to wine-based drinks and cordials.

COOKING AND EATING Pour a bottle of a medium red wine such as claret into a jug, add 2 tbsp caster sugar and the grated rind of a lemon. Stir and chill for one hour. Add a small glass of medium sherry or brandy, a few leaves each of Lemon Balm and of Borage, and a bottle of soda water. Add some Borage flowers for decoration and serve. An even more refreshing drink may be made by substituting cider for the wine, brandy and sherry, and adding slices of apple and pear. The young leaves can also be used in salads, though they are rather hairy and rough. This roughness is lost however, if they are cooked briefly like spinach and used with cream cheese as a pasta filling. The flowers make a highly decorative addition to salads and all kinds of other dishes, and may be rendered pink for further variety if soaked in lemon juice first.

114

Borage *grows to about knee height along well-drained fields and in waste ground, often as a result of having escaped from cottage gardens. The densely hairy stems give the plant a frosted appearance, particularly visible when backlit by the sun.*

Borage

RANGE: Throughout Western and Southern Europe as far north as southern Britain.

HABITAT: Wasteland.

FLOWERING TIME: May to September.

Balm (Lemon Balm)

Balm (Lemon Balm)
Melissa officinalis

Flowers are formed in dense whorls around the leaf axils, but usually with only one or two flowers in a whorl open at the same time. Each white flower has two lips, the lower of which is divided into three lobes.

Use
Add a handful of Lemon Balm leaves to leeks when sautéing them for leek and potato soup. Supplement the stock with a little lemon juice. Serve with a swirl of cream and decorate with shredded Balm leaves.

Leaves in opposite pairs on square stems. They are more or less oval in outline, 2-3 cm long with regularly toothed margins and a slightly wrinkled, typically yellow-green surface.

Hedgerows

Balm is native to the Mediterranean region, but has been cultivated for centuries elsewhere and is common of shady waste places wherever the climate is warm enough to support it. The name Melissa comes from the Greek for 'bee', signifying how strongly the flowers attract bees, indeed Balm was often planted close to beehives – it was thought that the scent would help bees find their way home.

COOKING AND EATING Balm is most famously used for making a refreshing tea, said to aid long life and dispel melancholy. Simply pour boiling water over a few leaves and allow the flavour to infuse. Lemon Balm tea is, however, only the start: the plant's subtle flavour, without the harshness or acidity of real lemon, can brighten up fish, salads, mayonnaise, eggs, poultry and sauces, especially cream sauces. Try a snack of left-over cold chicken by mixing it with mayonnaise, garlic, black pepper and mashed Lemon Balm leaves. Or add some chopped Balm to the Raspberry *coulis* recipe on page 90 and mixing in a little thick double cream with a spoonful of honey. Prepare a Balm pesto with 2 cups of leaves, half a cup of quality olive oil and two or more garlic cloves, blended together to a coarse finish – perfect for basting poultry or barbequed fish.

Balm *is a tufted perennial growing to waist height, though often much smaller. It looks rather like a yellowish-green mint, with small, neat leaves and a scattering of small flowers along its erect branches. Its lemon fragrance is only revealed when the leaves are rubbed between the fingers.*

Balm

RANGE: Throughout Europe except for northern Britain and northern Scandinavia.

HABITAT: Shady waste places, dry banks and hedgerows, often near human habitation.

FLOWERING TIME: July to September.

117

Water Mint

Water Mint
Mentha aquatica

Use
Make a delicious, refreshing mint tea by adding 4 or 5 Water Mint leaves to a pot of ordinary tea. Serve in a glass with plenty of sugar, a little lemon juice and decorate with a fresh Mint leaf and Borage flower.

The small 2-lipped flowers have protruding stamens, and are very densely clustered around the upper leaves or at the top of the stem. They may be pink or lilac.

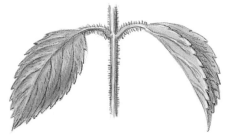

The delicate leaves, in opposite pairs, are pale green or flushed with bronze, and coarsely toothed.

Marshland

On hot, sunny days the air is refreshed in marshy meadows by the sweet scent of Water Mint, but if the leaves are picked and crushed in the hand the fragrance can be very-powerful and almost sickly. It grows luxuriantly wherever the ground is permanently moist, in swamps and on the margins of rivers and ditches. It may grow tall where there is lush waterside growth, and can be recognized by the domed clusters of flowers at the top of the plant, which vary between pink or distinctly lilac, in which case the leaves take on a bronzy hue.

COOKING AND EATING Water Mint can be used exactly like garden mint, which is one of a number of hybrids and cultivars of species that can be found growing wild, though Water Mint is by far the most common. As with many herbs, the potency of the flavour in the leaves is dependent on sunshine, so it is stronger in high summer. It makes an excellent *salsa verde* to serve with robust-tasting fish, such as tuna, bass or mullet. Using a mortar and pestle (or a blender for a smoother result), mix together 1 cup of chopped parsley, 1 cup of chopped Water Mint, a clove of garlic, 1 tablespoon of lemon juice and 1 teaspoon of Dijon mustard with half a cup of olive oil.

Water Mint *is very distinctive. It often grows up to knee-height, with plenty of bushy growth and clearly red-tinged leaves that release their fragrance as they are brushed past. The leaves are easily identified by their strong fragrance, even when the plant is not in flower.*

Water Mint

RANGE: Throughout Europe, except the far north.

HABITAT: Marshland, margins of rivers and ditches.

FLOWERING TIME: July to September.

Wild Marjoram

Wild Marjoram
Origanum vulgare

Use
Marinate some chopped Wild Marjoram leaves in olive oil with black pepper, salt and a little lemon juice for a few hours, then spoon generously over fresh, very ripe sliced tomatoes.

Leaves are pale green and untoothed, and are connected by fairly long stalks to the rigid purple stem. They have a strong herby smell.

The many, densely packed sprays of pink (occasionally white) flowers are surrounded by crimson bracts, giving a very colourful effect.

Grassy meadows

Wild Marjoram is a small, bushy plant, occurring in the driest grasslands and on roadsides, usually on limestone or chalky soils. It produces wide, spreading sprays of pink flowers, which are a favourite for their nectar with butterflies, and in particular with the day-flying, red-spotted burnet moths. Wild Marjoram is the source of culinary Oregano, and its smell is instantly recognizable if the leaves are rubbed, but in more northerly latitudes the fragrance is not as strong as in the Mediterranean sunshine.

COOKING AND EATING It goes particularly well with meat and can be added to stews and casseroles; a few leaves mixed in to the dough gives an earthy, rustic flavour to dumplings. For a typically Mediterranean pasta dish, gently fry some chopped smoked bacon or pancetta, with a few mushrooms (preferably wild), garlic, black pepper and a little chilli, in olive oil. Meanwhile, cook some ribbon pasta, such as spaghetti or linguine. In a separate pan, rapidly boil a can of chopped tomatoes with half a glass of red wine until reduced by half. One minute before serving, add some chopped wild marjoram leaves to the bacon, then add the tomatoes and the drained pasta to the pan and mix thoroughly. Serve with grated Parmesan cheese and a glass of full-bodied red wine.

Wild Marjoram *grows as a knee-high, bushy plant, producing foaming masses of pink and crimson flowers in the dry grassland of limestone hills. Use the leaves fresh, or hang up the stalks until the leaves have dried thoroughly and store them for later use.*

Wild Marjoram

RANGE: Throughout Europe, except the far north.

HABITAT: Dry grassland, roadsides.

FLOWERING TIME: July to September.

Wild Thyme

Wild Thyme
Thymus polytrichus

Use
Olives that have been preserved in oil can be given an extra lift by adding to the jar a few sprigs of thyme leaves and flowering tops, and some chopped cloves of garlic.

Bright pink flowers are in tight, rounded clusters, each with two lips but appearing to have four rounded petals. The plant often produces masses of blooms.

The leaves are tiny, just 4-8 mm long, simple in shape and in opposite pairs on the square stems (see left), which have hairs on opposing faces.

Breckland Thyme
(Thymus serpyllum)
has rounded stems with a fine covering of hairs, though a hand lens is needed to see them.

Grassy meadows

Wild Thyme generally keeps close to the ground and prefers well-drained turf in sunny situations, on either chalky or sandy soils or even on shingle. The thyme we associate with the kitchen garden is another species, *Thymus vulgaris*, which originates in the Mediterranean region and is a more bushy plant with upright stems, though there are many other varieties available with citrus-like scents or variegated leaves. Wild Thyme was often a component of the posy, originally a device to protect from infectious diseases, and the plant does contain a high proportion of thymol, a powerful antiseptic. In eastern and northern Europe this species is replaced by the almost identical Breckland Thyme (*Thymus serpyllum*), which has rounded stems rather than square.

COOKING AND EATING Thyme has a warm but pungent aroma, and works best with foods that are cooked slowly. It is a little too powerful for most fish dishes, but works very well with poultry, and a roast chicken can be greatly improved by its use. Strip the leaves of Wild Thyme from their stems and grind them into some softened butter with a single clove of garlic and a little black pepper. Gently pull the skin away from the breast of the bird and stuff with the butter mixture before roasting.

Wild Thyme *forms low cushions among short turf on dry soils. It is difficult to spot when not in flower, but otherwise produces an abundance of clustered pink flowers. When the plant's leaves are crushed, the scent of thyme is released, although it is not the species grown for culinary use.*

Wild Thyme

RANGE: Western and southern Europe.

HABITAT: Grassy meadows.

FLOWERING TIME: May to September.

Chanterelle

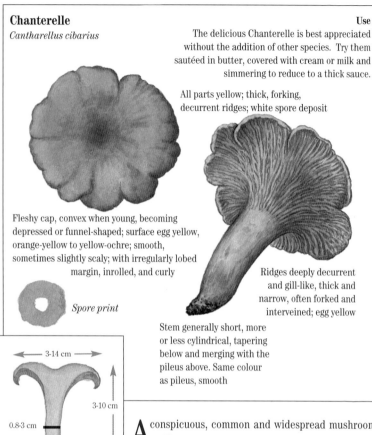

Chanterelle

Cantharellus cibarius

Use

The delicious Chanterelle is best appreciated without the addition of other species. Try them sautéed in butter, covered with cream or milk and simmering to reduce to a thick sauce.

All parts yellow; thick, forking, decurrent ridges; white spore deposit

Fleshy cap, convex when young, becoming depressed or funnel-shaped; surface egg yellow, orange-yellow to yellow-ochre; smooth, sometimes slightly scaly; with irregularly lobed margin, inrolled, and curly

Spore print

Ridges deeply decurrent and gill-like, thick and narrow, often forked and intervened; egg yellow

Stem generally short, more or less cylindrical, tapering below and merging with the pileus above. Same colour as pileus, smooth

3-14 cm

3-10 cm

0.8-3 cm

A conspicuous, common and widespread mushroom, and long considered one of the best edible varieties. It needs plenty of rain and prefers acid soils, often to be found glowing bright orange on a carpet of green moss beneath Beech trees. Take care not to confuse this with the False Chanterelle which always grows under conifers and has true gills.

COOKING AND EATING The smell is often somewhat fancifully likened to apricots, though the colour and the texture is certainly reminiscent of the fruit. This North African-inspired recipe makes full advantage of that quality, replacing the real apricots that would normally be used. Cut some good quality lamb leg-steaks into cubes and fry gently, with a little ground coriander seed, until they are cooked but still tender, and set aside to rest. In a separate pan fry some very roughly chopped Chanterelles with a little garlic and sliced red pepper. Then add 2 cups of good vegetable stock and simmer for ten minutes, adding some frozen peas halfway through. Bring the stock to a brisk boil and add 1 cup of dry couscous, stir and remove from the heat. Throw in a handful of blanched, halved almonds and plump sultanas, cover and leave for ten minutes. Check the seasoning, add some chopped Coriander leaf, fluff up the couscous with a fork and serve with the lamb on top.

Habitat: *On the ground in moist, broadleaved and coniferous woodland, often by the edge of paths on the ground; considered to have a broad host range, and is found among oak, beech, birch, spruce and pine.*

LOOKALIKES

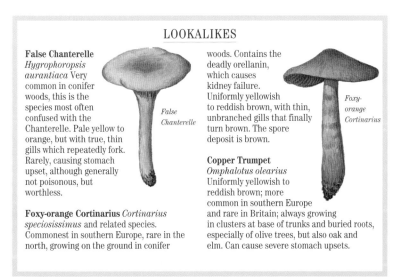

False Chanterelle
Hygrophoropsis aurantiaca Very common in conifer woods, this is the species most often confused with the Chanterelle. Pale yellow to orange, but with true, thin gills which repeatedly fork. Rarely, causing stomach upset, although generally not poisonous, but worthless.

False Chanterelle

Foxy-orange Cortinarius *Cortinarius speciosissimus* and related species. Commonest in southern Europe, rare in the north, growing on the ground in conifer woods. Contains the deadly orellanin, which causes kidney failure. Uniformly yellowish to reddish brown, with thin, unbranched gills that finally turn brown. The spore deposit is brown.

Foxy-orange Cortinarius

Copper Trumpet
Omphalotus olearius Uniformly yellowish to reddish brown; more common in southern Europe and rare in Britain; always growing in clusters at base of trunks and buried roots, especially of olive trees, but also oak and elm. Can cause severe stomach upsets.

125

Horse Mushroom

Horse Mushroom
Agaricus arvensis

Use
Horse Mushrooms have a faint smell of aniseed or bitter almonds, but this hardly affects their true mushroomy flavour.

Large and fleshy, white cap and stem which bruise yellowish; gills grey to blackish brown; stem with a large ring

Gills free, of several sizes and crowded, at first grey then blackish-brown

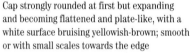

Cap strongly rounded at first but expanding and becoming flattened and plate-like, with a white surface bruising yellowish-brown; smooth or with small scales towards the edge

Spore print

Stem smooth and white, but bruising yellowish-brown, with a large, hanging, membranous, white ring towards the top, with cogwheel-like scales on the underside

7–15 cm

7–12 cm

1–2 cm

The name 'horse' has nothing to do with the animal: it is an old term indicating the large size. It is a glorious sight to find these monsters pushing their way up the through the lush grass of pastures in early autumn; they are often more common than the Field Mushroom (page 198). Take care not to confuse them with the poisonous Yellow Stainer (see Lookalikes). The white surfaces gradually discolour yellowish-brown as the mushrooms mature; pick them when the gills are greyish, before they turn dark brown with spores.

COOKING AND EATING Take advantage of their firm flesh and cook them whole. Allow one per person. First make a stuffing: slit the skins of some fresh chestnuts and boil for 15 minutes before peeling and chopping them. Mix these with twice their volume of breadcrumbs, a beaten egg and a knob of butter; season with salt, pepper and some chopped Wild Marjoram. Brush both sides of the caps with melted butter and fill them with the stuffing, topping off with a little grated cheese. Bake in a moderate oven for 20–25 minutes. Serve on toast, with steamed ground elder and dandelion leaves.

Habitat: In fields and pastures during the autumn.

LOOKALIKES

St. George's Mushroom
Calocybe gambosa Grows in similar grassland localities but is found only in the springtime. ***See page 62***

Yellow Stainer
Agaricus xanthoderma Take great care to avoid confusing this large, white, true mushroom, with horse mushroom, which it closely resembles; it can cause serious stomach upsets or even coma. The white surface of the cap and base of the stem of this mushroom *immediately* turns vivid yellow when it is cut or torn open. Usually grows under trees and has a strong, unpleasant smell of carbolic.

Destroying Angel
Amanita virosa A species growing in small numbers in leafy woodland, unlikely to be found in the open, preferring mountainous locations; it has white gills and spore deposit, a scaly stem which emerges from a white, sack-like volva; deadly poisonous, containing amatoxins.

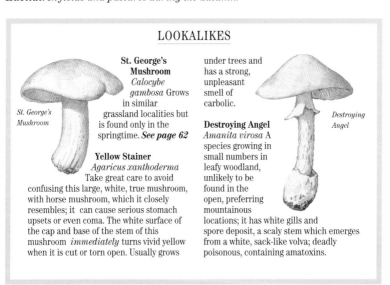

St. George's Mushroom

Destroying Angel

Chicken of the Woods

Chicken of the Woods
Laetiporus sulphureus

Overlapping sulphur yellow
brackets on trunks of trees

Cap fan-shaped, flattened, with an orange, lemon
yellow or sulphur yellow surface becoming paler and
whitish when old except for the margin, smooth

Use
This fungus makes superb kebabs. Cut the flesh
into cubes, marinate for 1 hour in seasoned lemon
juice and oil, then grill for 10 minutes. Serve with
a nutty sauce over rice or couscous.

Spore print

5-20 cm

Tubes forming a narrow layer, about 4
mm deep; pores small, 3-5 per mm,
round, sulphur yellow. No stem.

D istinctive, yellow brackets separate this species from
other bracket fungi. It forms tiers of layers on living
tree trunks, often tantalisingly out of reach, and is easily
spotted and recognised. It usually appears quite early in
the summer, and this is the best time to take advantage
of these fungi. Only young specimens should be eaten, when they are still orange or
bright sulphur-yellow, and have a firm, not hard texture. As it matures, the fungus
becomes hard and the colour seeps out of it, until it becomes almost white. It is widely eaten and very popular, especially in North America, but there are confirmed reports
that some people are allergic to it, suffering from serious gastric upset and sometimes
dizziness, on occasions within ten minutes of eating it. Therefore, sample only a small
portion when trying it for the first time, and never eat it raw. The colour and texture
of the flesh is reminiscent of chicken, and some liken the taste to poultry.

COOKING AND EATING It may be used as a replacement for chicken in many dishes,
such as in a cream sauce with pasta, or in a pie. It works very well in a casserole, with
or without meat such as pork or real chicken, and should be cut into cubes and added
to the pot to cook for the final 30 minutes.

Habitat: Clustered on trunks of living trees, preferring oak, sweet chestnut and yew; also reported on eucalyptus.

LOOKALIKES

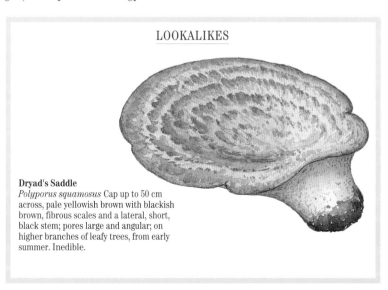

Dryad's Saddle
Polyporus squamosus Cap up to 50 cm across, pale yellowish brown with blackish brown, fibrous scales and a lateral, short, black stem; pores large and angular; on higher branches of leafy trees, from early summer. Inedible.

Edible Periwinkle

Edible Periwinkle
Littorina littorea

The colour is usually grey-brown or almost blackish, though sometimes reddish. They are always patterned with concentric, darker lines.

Eating

Eat your winkles one at a time, using a pin first to remove the operculum, which is the circular disc, like a little door to the shell opening. With a twisting, spiral action prise out the flesh from the shell with the pin, dip it in vinegar laced with plenty of white pepper.

The shell is generally 2.5-3 cm long, and sharply conical with a pointed apex. Young specimens may have a ridged surface, but older ones are usually worn smoother. The outer lip of the opening is more less parallel to the spire where the two meet.

The Rough Periwinkle (*Littorina saxatilis*) grows to only 1 cm, and is usually paler, with a rougher surface and outer lip meeting the spire almost at a right angle.

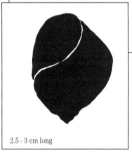

2.5 - 3 cm long

The Edible Periwinkle is one of the most common of edible shellfish and it is usually easy to gather a reasonable quantity in a good area. Any rocky coastline at low tide should reveal plenty, clinging to rocks either in or out of the water, and it is always worth turning over fronds of seaweed such as Bladderwrack or the related Toothed Wrack in case some are clinging beneath. Here too you may find the smaller Flat Periwinkle (*Littorina littoralis*), which is often brightly coloured yellow. Edible Periwinkles (or winkles) are the largest of several species, but nevertheless it is worth seeking out the largest of those for eating as they are very fiddly to deal with, usually on the lowest part of the shore. They do not need too much washing or purging: rinsing in fresh water is often enough, but those found in sandy areas may be left in fresh water overnight in order to remove any grit.

COOKING AND EATING Winkles do not have much flavour, and most of the fun of eating them is in 'winkling out' the flesh from the spiral shells. These should be plunged into salted, boiling water, and boiled for five minutes. The flavour may be improved by boiling them in vegetable stock, or by adding onion, leek, celery, carrot and herbs to the water, and allowing that to infuse for 15 minutes before adding the winkles.

Winkles *are common and easy to find on the lower tidal zone, between the mid- and low-water mark. They can survive out of water, so may be seen on the rocks themselves, as well as under water in rock pools. They are particularly fond of grazing on Brown Seaweeds, such as Bladderwrack.*

Edible Periwinkle

RANGE: Widespread throughout the region.

COLLECTING PERIOD: At any time.

Common Whelk

Common Whelk
Buccinum undatum

The shell is up to 10 cm long, fairly sharply conical with well-defined, rounded whorls which are lined and ribbed.

Gathering
Whelks can concentrate toxins in their gut, so be sure to collect them from the cleanest waters, well away from sewage outfalls, industrial outlets or other areas of human pollution.

Colour is pale brown or grey-brown.

The large aperture has a wide, pale lining with a notch or canal, which accommodates the siphon, through which the animal filter feeds.

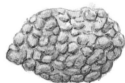

Rounded masses of empty Whelk egg capsules, like papery bubbles, are frequently washed up on the beach.

Up to 10cm long

The Whelk is a common and somewhat voracious, carnivorous feeder on other molluscs. They eat Mussels and other shellfish either by attacking them when their flesh is exposed, or by boring a hole through their shells. They will also eat carrion, and can be tempted into simple 'lobster-style' pots with a suitable bait of fish heads or crushed mussels. Empty Whelk shells frequently wash up on the shore, and may be taken up as temporary homes by small hermit crabs. Even commoner are their empty egg cases, like masses of spongy bubbles.

Whelks are a love-it-or-hate-it food – the rubbery texture of the flesh is not to everyone's taste. They do not have a strong flavour, so if eaten plain there is a tendency to concentrate a little too much on the texture. They are greatly improved by adding as much flavour as possible in cooking.

COOKING AND EATING Clean the Whelks by leaving them in fresh water for several hours, and scrubbing off any algae or other growths on their shells. Plunge them into rapidly boiling, well-salted water, to which has been added an onion, a carrot, celery, bay leaves and a glass of white wine. Simmer for about ten minutes, then tease them out of their shells using a stout needle, discarding the slimy portion at the 'tail' end. Serve with a richly-flavoured cream sauce, or mayonnaise laced with garlic and parsley.

The Common Whelk lives mostly just below the low water mark, but may be found in rock pools at low tide, especially those with sandy or gravelly bottoms. They may be in company with Dog Whelks, a much smaller species which is generally more colourful, with darker coloured bands. Here they can be seen producing their eggs.

Common Whelk

RANGE: Mainly a northern species, found in the Atlantic, English Channel, North Sea, and western Baltic areas.

COLLECTING PERIOD: At any time, but safest in colder months.

Garden Snail

Garden Snail
Helix aspersa

Tip
Snails collected from their hibernation in the period mid-winter to early spring do not need to be purged, since they are already starved. Look for them under pieces of wood, stones, or upturned buckets.

The coiled shell is up to 40 mm wide, pale brown in colour with up to five darker bands. Body colour is usually dark grey, though sometimes lighter.

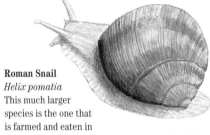

Roman Snail
Helix pomatia
This much larger species is the one that is farmed and eaten in restaurants. It has a creamy-coloured shell with less pronounced banding, up to 50 mm wide. It lives on chalk and limestone grassland, but is becoming rare so should not be collected from the wild. It is a protected species in Britain.

Up to 40mm across shell

The Garden Snail is a familiar to everyone, yet this extremely common food resource is greatly underused. They are successful creatures, able to take advantage of a wide range of food sources, and survive in many climates, simply retreating into hibernation if it is too cold or too dry. They are not to everyone's taste, but can be improved greatly with the addition of a strongly-flavoured sauce.

Cooking and eating Snails gathered in summer do need to be purged, so that any half-digested vegetation remaining in their gut is removed. Put them in a snail-proof container (a large bowl with a tight-fitting chicken-wire lid is ideal for this), and feed them on a diet of clean lettuce leaves for five days. They then need to be starved for two days, so that the last of this 'clean food' leaves their digestive systems, before they are cooked and eaten.

Once they are ready they need to be chilled in the refrigerator or freezer, and then thrown straight into rapidly boiling water to cook – make sure they have retreated back into their shells before doing this. Remove them with a pin, in the manner of winkles or whelks, and toss in salt. Add them to risottos, or a garlic, cream and wine sauce, or toss in garlic butter and return them to their shells for serving.

The **Garden Snail** can be found almost anywhere that is damp and sheltered, with plenty of soft leaves available as food, so gardens are ideal. On damp summer nights they can be heard squelching through the undergrowth, or found during the day sheltering under stones, leaves and garden paraphernalia.

Garden Snail

RANGE: Throughout Europe.

COLLECTING PERIOD: At any time.

Common Prawn

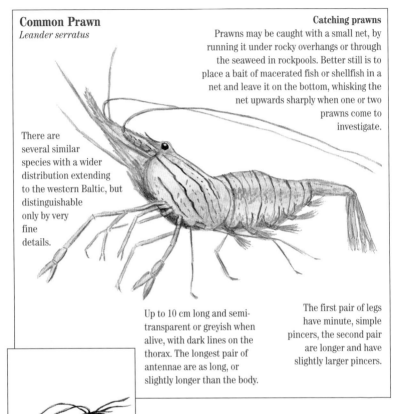

Common Prawn
Leander serratus

There are several similar species with a wider distribution extending to the western Baltic, but distinguishable only by very fine details.

Catching prawns
Prawns may be caught with a small net, by running it under rocky overhangs or through the seaweed in rockpools. Better still is to place a bait of macerated fish or shellfish in a net and leave it on the bottom, whisking the net upwards sharply when one or two prawns come to investigate.

Up to 10 cm long and semi-transparent or greyish when alive, with dark lines on the thorax. The longest pair of antennae are as long, or slightly longer than the body.

The first pair of legs have minute, simple pincers, the second pair are longer and have slightly larger pincers.

Up to 10cm long

Prawns are such a familiar sight in supermarkets, the bright pink shells piled up on the freezer counter, that it may come as something of a surprise to see the almost transparent living creature. It is difficult to predict exactly which spots are likely to be good prawn-hunting territory, but, unlike Shrimps, they prefer rocky habitats with plenty of hiding places and seaweed.

COOKING AND EATING Prawns should be cooked by plunging them directly into boiling, salted water. Two minutes is usually enough: over-cooking makes them shrink, so the meat becomes tough. The size of prawns caught on the shore is unlikely to match those caught out in the open sea, and you won't get large numbers. Perhaps for this reason they are best enjoyed straight away, as a snack cooked on the beach, dipping the meat into a bowl of olive oil and garlic, or sunflower oil, chilli and sugar. To catch as many as possible, buy a collapsible prawn trap from a sea-angling shop. This can then be left in place, firmly anchored to some heavy stones, until exposed at the next low tide, when you revisit to claim your catch. Bait the trap with some dead fish, and expect to find that whelks and small crabs have also been attracted by the scent.

Prawns *prefer rocky areas where they can hide in nooks and crannies, or among green seaweeds. They frequently become trapped in rock pools by the retreating tide, but may need to be coaxed out of hiding with a suitable bait of a crushed limpet or something similar. This is a female, carrying eggs.*

Common Prawn

RANGE: The Mediterranean, Atlantic, and English Channel.

COLLECTING PERIOD: At any time, but most common in late summer.

Common Shrimp

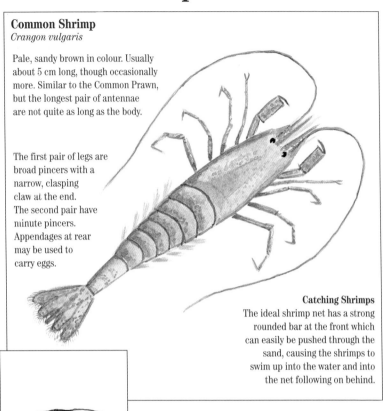

Common Shrimp
Crangon vulgaris

Pale, sandy brown in colour. Usually about 5 cm long, though occasionally more. Similar to the Common Prawn, but the longest pair of antennae are not quite as long as the body.

The first pair of legs are broad pincers with a narrow, clasping claw at the end. The second pair have minute pincers. Appendages at rear may be used to carry eggs.

Catching Shrimps
The ideal shrimp net has a strong rounded bar at the front which can easily be pushed through the sand, causing the shrimps to swim up into the water and into the net following on behind.

Around 5 cm long

Shrimps are very similar in many ways to Prawns, but have a different lifestyle – instead of wandering among rocks, they bury themselves in sand. They will sometimes reveal themselves if the surface is disturbed a little, scooting along for a short distance before burying themselves again, using their tails to pull themselves down backwards into the sand. They can only be caught with a net, and you won't get worthwhile numbers unless you buy a proper shrimping net, incorporating a bar at the front that can be pushed through the sand a few centimetres below the surface, making the Shrimps swim up above the sand, and into the net.

COOKING AND EATING They should be kept in sea water for as short a time as possible before cooking, which should be done in clean sea water, or water with 30 g of salt added per litre. Bring the water to a rolling boil, and plunge the Shrimps straight in. Cook them for no more than two or three minutes, when they will turn pinkish-brown. Cool them off in cold water and peel – a very fiddly business. Eat them in a wild green salad with a rich dressing, or make potted shrimps by mixing 200 g of peeled Shrimps with 50 g of melted butter, a pinch of mace and a pinch of cayenne pepper, pouring into little pots and cooling in the refrigerator.

The Common Shrimp *occurs on the tidal zone, just below the sand surface, but only where covered with water. So, search for them in large rock pools with sandy bottoms, or in sand pools or the shallows of the sea, provided it is calm.*

Common Shrimp

RANGE: Throughout in the Mediterranean, Atlantic, English Channel, North Sea and Baltic.

COLLECTING PERIOD: At any time.

Signal Crayfish

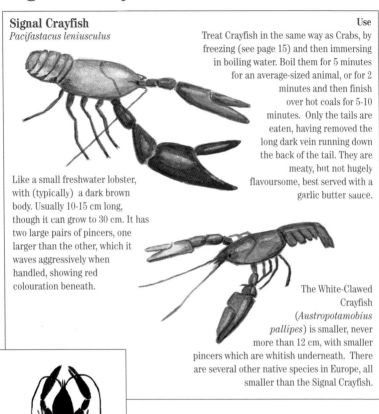

Signal Crayfish

Pacifastacus leniusculus

Like a small freshwater lobster, with (typically) a dark brown body. Usually 10-15 cm long, though it can grow to 30 cm. It has two large pairs of pincers, one larger than the other, which it waves aggressively when handled, showing red colouration beneath.

Up to 30 cm long

Use

Treat Crayfish in the same way as Crabs, by freezing (see page 15) and then immersing in boiling water. Boil them for 5 minutes for an average-sized animal, or for 2 minutes and then finish over hot coals for 5-10 minutes. Only the tails are eaten, having removed the long dark vein running down the back of the tail. They are meaty, but not hugely flavoursome, best served with a garlic butter sauce.

The White-Clawed Crayfish (*Austropotamobius pallipes*) is smaller, never more than 12 cm, with smaller pincers which are whitish underneath. There are several other native species in Europe, all smaller than the Signal Crayfish.

The Signal Crayfish, a freshwater crustacean, was introduced into Europe from North America in the 1970s for commercial production. Inevitably, a few escaped into the wild, and these have proliferated so much that they are regarded as a serious pest. They burrow into the banks of streams and rivers, causing serious damage, and damaging wild fish stocks by eating their eggs. Even more seriously, they have decimated the numbers of the native White-Clawed Crayfish (*Austropotamobius pallipes*), through direct competition for food, aggressive behaviour, and by spreading a fungal disease called crayfish plague. The White-Clawed Crayfish is a protected species in much of Europe, and must not be taken from the wild. Catching Signal Crayfish, on the other hand, is often encouraged, but a licence is needed in some countries, and there are laws regarding the transportation and handling of live specimens, so check with your local environmental authority beforehand.

COOKING AND EATING They can often be caught with a bait of fish or chicken meat on a piece of string, or alternatively can be hooked out of the water with a net. Crayfish traps are also available, which can be highly effective in areas where there are high numbers of Crayfish.

The Signal Crayfish can often be seen wandering over the beds of shallow freshwater streams, ponds and rivers. Sometimes their burrows can be seen in the bank below the water's surface. Be sure to correctly identify the species before removing them – in many countries it is illegal to take other, native species.

Signal Crayfish

RANGE: Throughout most of Europe.

COLLECTING PERIOD: April to October, otherwise in hibernation.

Shore Crab

Shore Crab
Carcinus maenas

Other, slightly similar species have either seven projecting teeth either side of the carapace, or rounded 'paddles' on the last pair of legs – an adaptation for swimming.

Tip
Try to avoid keeping several Shore Crabs in each other's company for too long, as they are apt to attack each other. It's a fiddly job but you could try putting a rubber band around each pincer, or simply keep them separate.

The body colour is olive or dark green, occasionally brownish, and yellow-green below. They are 6-8 cm across, though often much smaller. There are three small teeth on the margin of the carapace between the eyes, and five sharply pointed teeth on either side of the body. The first pair of legs bear smallish, equal-sized pincers, which are nevertheless powerful. The fifth (last) pair of legs have flattened joints, the last joint being pointed.

Up to 8 cm across shell

Shore Crabs are eminently edible and have a very good flavour, the only problem being their small size. The smallest ones should be left alone to mature and breed, but larger ones are worth collecting. They can be simply picked up, or tempted out of hiding in rock pools with a suitable bait of fish meat, or fished for off piers and sea walls with bait tied to a weighted line. They will usually hang on to the bait at least until out of the water so a landing net may be useful. Refer to the introduction (page 15) for notes on killing crabs, which is best done as soon as possible. Any algae, seaweeds or sponges sticking to the surface of the carapace should be scrubbed off with a nail brush.

COOKING AND EATING The small size of most Shore Crabs makes them excellent for a crab bisque. Cook about 800 g crabs in well-salted water for 5 minutes, then remove and chop roughly with a heavy knife. Sauté in butter some onion, carrot and celery, then add the crab, 2 tbsp brandy, a can of chopped tomatoes, some tarragon, a glass of wine and 1 and a half litres of fish stock. Simmer for 30 minutes. Remove the crab claws from the broth, and roughly process the broth, shells included, in a liquidizer to break up the shell (but not pulverise it) and release the meat. Strain the liquid twice, bring back to boil and add 50 ml double cream, a squeeze of lemon juice and seasoning.

Shore Crabs *are by far the most common species likely to be encountered on the shore, in rock pools, under stones or around the base of piers, jetties and breakwaters. In spite of their small size they can be quite aggressive, so handle with caution, picking them up from the rear.*

Shore Crab

RANGE: Throughout the region in the Mediterranean, Atlantic, English Channel, North Sea and the Baltic.

COLLECTING PERIOD: At any time, but most common in late summer.

Edible Crab

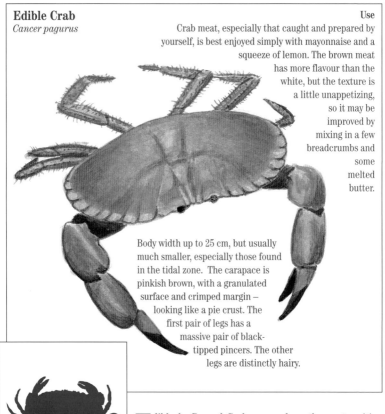

Edible Crab
Cancer pagurus

Use
Crab meat, especially that caught and prepared by yourself, is best enjoyed simply with mayonnaise and a squeeze of lemon. The brown meat has more flavour than the white, but the texture is a little unappetizing, so it may be improved by mixing in a few breadcrumbs and some melted butter.

Body width up to 25 cm, but usually much smaller, especially those found in the tidal zone. The carapace is pinkish brown, with a granulated surface and crimped margin – looking like a pie crust. The first pair of legs has a massive pair of black-tipped pincers. The other legs are distinctly hairy.

Up to 25 cm wide

Edible (or Brown) Crabs are perhaps the most exciting find that can be made on the shoreline, though it is more likely to be a matter of chance rather than the outcome of deliberate searching. Small specimens do frequent the lower shore, but it is better to leave anything under 10 cm wide to mature and breed. Having caught one, it is necessary to kill it, referring to the notes in the introduction, and prepare it as soon as possible.

COOKING AND EATING Crabs up to 1 kg need to be boiled in very salty water for about 15 minutes, adding another five minutes for every extra 500 g. When cool, twist off the legs and pincers. Turn the crab on its back, pull back the pointed tail flap and remove. Insert a strong knife under the leg joints, where the main shell meets the undershell, and prise the two apart, levering up with the thumbs if necessary. Pull away the mouthparts and the stomach sac in one piece and discard. Then pull away the grey gills, ('dead man's fingers') and discard (these are not poisonous – simply inedible). What remains inside the shell is all edible meat, and needs to be spooned out with whatever tools you have. To get out the delicious white meat inside the pincers and legs, crack them with nutcrackers or by wrapping them in cloth and tapping with a rolling pin.

Edible Crabs *are sometimes (if you are lucky) stranded in rock pools by the retreating tide, especially in very rocky areas. They are likely to be hiding in nooks and crannies and may be tempted out with a piece of fish bait. Large specimens are usually only encountered in deep water.*

Edible Crab

RANGE: The Mediterranean, Atlantic, English
Channel and North Sea.

COLLECTING PERIOD: At any time, but most
common in summer.

145

Spiny Spider Crab

Spiny Spider Crab
Maia squinado

Use
Spider Crab meat can be used in any recipe calling for edible crab meat, and is regarded as having the best flavour. It is particularly good in a pasta dish dressed with a simple sauce of tomatoes, garlic and chilli, or in fish cakes.

The carapace is reddish-orange like the legs, but this is often obscured by barnacles, seaweed and sponges which the crab uses as camouflage.

Very long reddish-orange legs characterise this species. The first pair of legs end in moderately-sized claws. The carapace is longer than it is broad, and more or less triangular, with short (and longer) spines around the margin, and two long forward-projecting spines between the eyes. The carapace may be up to 18 cm long, but this is exceptional.

Up to 18 cm long

Spider Crabs are somewhat forbidding-looking creatures, as their exceptionally long legs wave wildly in the air when picked up, though they are not as fierce as their appearance suggests. The meat is very good to eat, and acknowledged by many to be as good or even better than lobster. They are fairly common in warm waters, scrambling over rocks just below the lower shore, but sometimes they become trapped in rock pools during the lowest tides so it is always worth searching for them. They may also be caught readily in crab pots, which should be left in position for 24 hours, baited with fish meat. The pot should be tied to an immovable object as far down the shore as possible, and checked at the next low tide.

Cooking and eating Spider Crabs should be killed in the same way as other crabs, by freezing and then sudden boiling, as described in the introduction. Allow at least 15 minutes for the flesh to be cooked in boiling, salted water, adding another 5 minutes for every 500 g above 1 kg in weight. The white meat is exceptionally sweet, worth the effort of extracting every morsel from the narrow claws. Prepare the animal in the same way as the Edible Crab (page 144), discarding the inedible stomach sac and gills.

Spider Crabs *may occasionally be found in rock pools and reefs at low tide. They are not easy to spot, as their bodies are often covered with seaweed and sponges, and can look exactly like a piece of rock. The long legs and pincers poking out from an overhang are the best clue.*

Spiny Spider Crab

RANGE: found in the Mediterranean, Atlantic and English Channel. A southern species.

COLLECTING PERIOD: At any time, but best from May to December.

Autumn

Of course, this is the season of greatest abundance. Make the most of it by gathering bucketfuls of fruit and turning them into jams, jellies and sauces. You'll need to be quick to beat the birds and mice, but don't worry too much about depriving them of their food: unless you are running a commercial enterprise with teams of pickers, collecting for home use is no more than a scratch on the surface.

The mushrooming season has already begun, so learn to identify them while you have the chance, and dry or freeze what you can't eat straight away.

◁ *Blackberry*

Dog Rose

Honey Fungus

Cauliflower Fungus

Hawthorn

Juniper

Juniper
Juniperus communis

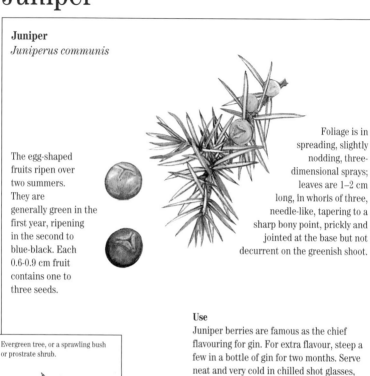

The egg-shaped fruits ripen over two summers. They are generally green in the first year, ripening in the second to blue-black. Each 0.6-0.9 cm fruit contains one to three seeds.

Foliage is in spreading, slightly nodding, three-dimensional sprays; leaves are 1–2 cm long, in whorls of three, needle-like, tapering to a sharp bony point, prickly and jointed at the base but not decurrent on the greenish shoot.

Evergreen tree, or a sprawling bush or prostrate shrub.

to 8 m

Use
Juniper berries are famous as the chief flavouring for gin. For extra flavour, steep a few in a bottle of gin for two months. Serve neat and very cold in chilled shot glasses, with a fresh berry floating on top

Juniper is the most widely distributed tree species, occurring throughout the northern temperate region. It usually forms a shrub rather than a tree, and can tolerate a wide range of soil conditions from chalk or limestone hills to acid peats. When heated over a fire, the wood produces a fragrant smoke which is used to smoke fish and other meats. Juniper is an evergreen conifer tree species, and the 'berries' it produces are actually small fleshy cones. They are green in their first year, but do not ripen until their second, when they turn blue-black and develop a waxy bloom.

COOKING AND EATING The berries are quite bitter and can be roasted and ground and used as a coffee substitute. The flavour marries well with casseroled game, such as rabbit, pheasant or venison. Tie a rasher of streaky bacon around some rabbit pieces and sear them in a casserole until browned. Remove the rabbit and sautée some onion in a little oil until soft. Replace the rabbit, add some crushed Juniper berries, a bayleaf, half a glass of dry sherry and some chicken stock to cover. Cook in a moderate oven for 45–60 minutes. Remove the meat to rest, strain the liquid and boil to reduce. Finally, whisk in some butter and parsley. Serve with roast potatoes for a warming dish.

Juniper occurs in many habit forms, often in the same locality. This specimen is typical – it is a scrubby tree at the best of times.

BARK
Reddish-brown, on older trees developing papery scales.

Hawthorn

Hawthorn
Crataegus monogyna

Use
Make Hawthorn schnapps by filling a clean jar two thirds with washed haws, and then covering with vodka. Keep in a dark place for two months before bottling and serving with game or salmon.

The flowers are rose like, with five rounded white petals and pink anthers, and arranged in tight clusters.

The alternately-arranged leaves are oval or diamond-shaped in outline, but deeply divided into three or five sharp-toothed lobes. They are usually dark, glossy green and borne on viciously thorny shoots.

The egg-shaped fruit is a bright, glossy red, though sometimes a dark red, and consists of a single stone surrounded by rather dry, firm yellow flesh.

Deciduous tree or shrub

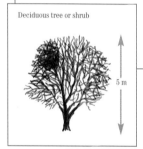

5 m

Hawthorn is a very common and widespread tree or shrub throughout; it is easy to confuse with a few very similar species, including the Azarole of the Mediterranean region, highly esteemed for its fruits. The young leaves of Hawthorn have a fresh, nutty taste, and make an excellent addition to salads. They need to be picked just after the buds have burst, before flowers have bloomed. The fruits or haws are perhaps the most abundant of all wild fruits, the trees are often scarlet with them in autumn.

COOKING AND EATING Hawthorn haws make a beautiful red jelly, but you need to use more water than usual in order to extract sufficient juice: at least one litre to every kilo of fruit. Allow 450 g of sugar to each 600 ml of juice extracted (following the recipe on page 20), and add the juice of a lemon to make extra pectin. Alternatively, an equal weight of haws and crab apples may be used, in which case the lemon is not necessary.

For a quicker result you can make Hawthorn sauce, which is excellent withroast pigeon breast. Gently simmer 650 g of fruit in 450 ml of white wine vinegar for 30 minutes, then strain the pulp through a sieve. Add 100 g of sugar to the juice and boil for 10 minutes until thickened, season with plenty of salt and black pepper.

Hawthorn forms a broadly spreading, domed tree or shrub, usually about 5 m high. Often in hedges, it is planted and trimmed to make an impenetrable, thorny tangle for enclosing livestock. It grows throughout Europe, except for northern Scandinavia, and flowers from April to June.

BARK
Orange- or grey-brown, becoming cracked and scaly with age and with rounded, longitudinal ridges.

153

Walnut

Walnut

Juglans regia

Yellow male catkins, 5–10 cm long, appear from lateral buds, with the new leaves. Female flowers are at the tips of the new shoots.

Use

Add ripe Walnut pieces to cooked cabbage or sea kale shoots, seasoned with butter, black pepper and nutmeg, for a warming winter vegetable.

Shoot stout, smooth dark brown. Split lengthwise, pith is seen chambered like ladder rungs. Buds egg-shaped, pointed, with two outer scales.

Fruit globe-shaped, enclosed in a thick green case. It splits on ripening in the first autumn to release the rugged, pointed nut (4–5 cm).

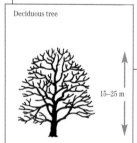

Pinnate leaves (divided into leaflets) alternate on the shoot, 20–45 cm long. They have 5 to 9 (rarely to 13) oval leaflets, 20 cm by 10 cm, but larger towards the leaf tip. Margin generally untoothed. Upper surface dull green, underside shiny light green with white tufts in the vein junctions.

Deciduous tree

15–25 m

Walnut is probably native to south-eastern Europe and into China, and still forms extensive pure forest in the states of the former Soviet Union (such as Azerbaijan). However, it has a long history of cultivation for its nuts, and is clearly an introduced tree in western Europe, despite often being called English Walnut. It is valued for its dark-brown, richly veined wood, long used for veneers and gun butts, but is rather scarce, except where it has been deliberately planted. The fruit can be harvested in summer before the nuts have begun to harden – this is the ideal time to pickle them.

COOKING AND EATING For sweet-pickled Walnuts, pare off the green outer skin – the hard shell inside has not yet formed. Prick the nuts with a fork to let the juice (which stains) run out, and cover them with a strong brine for two weeks, changing the brine once or twice. Allow the nuts to dry in a warm place for two days, when they turn black. Then prepare the pickling syrup of 1 litre malt vinegar, 500 g brown sugar, 4 cloves, some black peppercorns and a pinch of cinnamon. Boil up the syrup and simmer the Walnuts in it for 15 minutes, then seal in sterilized jars. The longer they are kept, the better they become.

Walnut makes a domed crown, usually with branches radiating out from a short bole, or trunk. It does not tolerate shade. The tree produces chemicals which inhibit the growth of other plants.

BARK
On young trees shiny, smooth and grey, developing smooth, broad ridges separated by wide, and deep fissures.

Hazel

Hazel
Corylus avellana

Use

Roast your own Hazelnuts in the oven at 135°C, or for spicy nuts, cover them with salt, brown sugar and cayenne pepper and roast at 175°C, turning them frequently and watching that they don't burn.

Fruit is the familiar brown nut, 1.5–2cm long, which is encased in a leafy, cup-like structure; often 2 or 3 are clustered together.

The leaves are rather hairy, broadly oval or heart-shaped, and quite small at first, but continuing to grow in size throughout the season until they reach about 10 cm long. The shoots are hairy when young.

Male catkins appear as early as October, but do not expand to produce clouds of yellow pollen until February or March. Female flowers are tiny, like 3-mm crimson stars at the tips of the green buds.

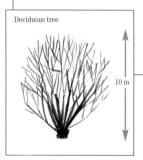

Deciduous tree

10 m

Hazel is a common tree or shrub found throughout most of Europe. In the past, a considerable rural industry built up around Hazel as a result of its tendency to produce slender stems from ground level. These are straight and very supple, and if cut on a regular 10–12 year cycle (coppicing) will go on producing the stems for many decades. These are split and woven into wattles and hurdles for fencing sheep, or were used in the past as the framework on which mud or plaster was daubed to make cottage walls. The twigs are used as dowsing rods by water diviners. The long, yellow male catkins appear before the leaves open, but the female flowers are tiny, with only the bright red stigmas showing. The highly nutritious nut (cobnut) contains up to 65 per cent oil, which can be used in paints and cosmetics, as well as for polishing wood. The nuts will keep for up to 12 months if left in their shells, but should be collected as early as possible, for they are taken by animals such as squirrels and dormice or by woodpeckers.

COOKING AND EATING An excellent pesto sauce can be made by blending 1 cup of Hazelnuts, half a cup of olive oil, a large bunch of parsley, 2 garlic cloves and black pepper. Serve with grilled fish or pasta.

Hazel usually grows either as an understorey layer in old broadleaved woodland, or in hedgerows, as a shrubby tree up to 10 m high, with several stems rising from the same point at ground level.

BARK
Shiny grey-brown and rather smooth, but peeling in strips.

Beech

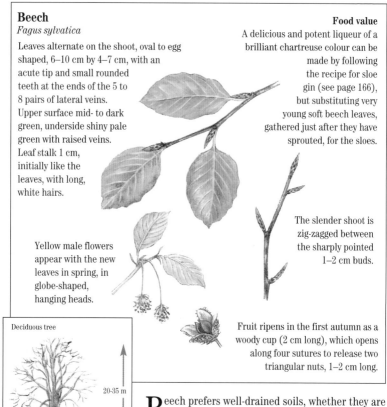

Beech

Fagus sylvatica

Leaves alternate on the shoot, oval to egg shaped, 6–10 cm by 4–7 cm, with an acute tip and small rounded teeth at the ends of the 5 to 8 pairs of lateral veins. Upper surface mid- to dark green, underside shiny pale green with raised veins. Leaf stalk 1 cm, initially like the leaves, with long, white hairs.

Yellow male flowers appear with the new leaves in spring, in globe-shaped, hanging heads.

Food value

A delicious and potent liqueur of a brilliant chartreuse colour can be made by following the recipe for sloe gin (see page 166), but substituting very young soft beech leaves, gathered just after they have sprouted, for the sloes.

The slender shoot is zig-zagged between the sharply pointed 1–2 cm buds.

Fruit ripens in the first autumn as a woody cup (2 cm long), which opens along four sutures to release two triangular nuts, 1–2 cm long.

Deciduous tree

20-35 m

Beech prefers well-drained soils, whether they are acid or alkaline. Established beech woods often have very little other green vegetation at ground level, since the dense shade cast by the leaves in summer prevents the strong growth of other plants. They are, however, excellent hunting grounds for autumn fungi.

Cooking and eating Collect the triangular nuts, or mast, just as the bristly husks start to open; if left for too long, squirrels and mice will take them all, or they disappear into the leaf litter. It is an extremely fiddly job to remove the tiny kernel from its shiny, brown leathery shell – best done with a small, sharp knife. For this reason, only a small amount can reasonably be harvested before one's patience expires. They do, however, have a delicious buttery flavour, and go well with other nuts to make vegetarian meatballs, or 'nutballs'. Mix together equal quantities of finely chopped beech nuts, hazel nuts and walnuts with breadcrumbs, grated celery, onion and carrot, a little grated cheese and some chopped parsley. Bind together with a little milk and an egg and shape into balls 3–4 cm across. Bake in a moderate oven until a skewer poked into the centre comes out clean. Serve with a tomato sauce and spaghetti.

Beech makes attractive specimen trees, as well as forming extensive forests. Nuts are enclosed in a woody bristly cup that splits open into four parts when the nuts are ripe. They are usually well out of reach, so diligent searching is required to find the nuts on the woodland floor.

BARK
Smooth and silvery grey throughout the life of most trees, although some occasionally become scaly at the base.

Sweet Chestnut

Sweet Chestnut
Castanea sativa

Oblong, lance shaped leaves, 15-20 cm by 7-10 cm alternate on the shoot. Lateral veins extend beyond the leaf margin to make regular bristles. Upper surface deep green, underside pale, with fine hairs. Leaf stalk 2.5-3.5 cm. The tree is one of the last to come into flower, and male flowers form at the ends of the current year's shoots in midsummer. The whitish yellow catkins expand to 12 cm; female flowers lie at the base of the catkins.

Use
To roast Chestnuts over an open fire, split some nuts with a sharp knife, place on a small shovel over hot coals. Ready in 10–15 minutes, they can be peeled and eaten immediately with butter and salt.

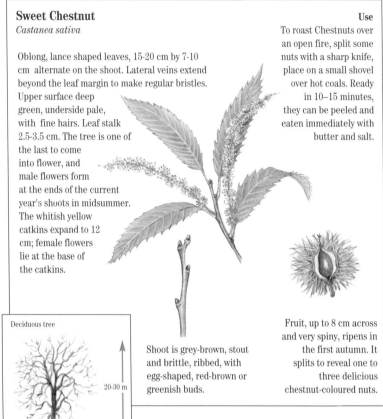

Deciduous tree

20-30 m

Shoot is grey-brown, stout and brittle, ribbed, with egg-shaped, red-brown or greenish buds.

Fruit, up to 8 cm across and very spiny, ripens in the first autumn. It splits to reveal one to three delicious chestnut-coloured nuts.

Sweet Chestnut has been widely planted throughout Europe for its valuable timber. The tree responds well to coppicing on a 10–12 year cycle to produce a regular growth of poles. The timber is almost as resilient as Oak to rotting in wet conditions and splits easily, so is used for making fence posts and rails, but the growth is too coarse for finer work. Sweet Chestnut makes unreliable firewood, except for in wood-burning stoves.

COOKING AND EATING Sweet Chestnuts can also be made into a purée, coated with syrup to make *marrons glacés*, used as flour, or boiled with Brussels sprouts. For chestnut stuffing, split two cups of chestnuts and boil them for 10 minutes so that they can be peeled easily. Boil for a little longer, once peeled, and mince them in a blender, then combine with 1 cup of pork sausage meat, half a cup of breadcrumbs, a beaten egg, salt and pepper. Sauté a little onion in some butter and add it to the mixture. Perfect for stuffing Christmas poultry.

Old Sweet Chestnuts, with their tall, domed crowns, can make attractive trees, although they often have a few suckers at their feet. Young trees are much more column shaped, with rather whorled branching.

BARK
Smooth and shiny grey on young trees, later developing fissures and ridges, which often spiral up the trunk.

Wild Service Tree

Wild Service Tree
Sorbus torminalis

Fruit is egg-shaped to globe-shaped, 1–1.5 cm, ripening to russet green or brown and covered with many small breathing pores (lenticels).

Leaves alternate on the shoots and are egg- shaped in outline, with a rounded, cut-off or a shallow heart-shape base. The leaves have a pair of triangular lobes near the base, and there are several small triangular lobes or large teeth which decrease in size towards the acute tip. Margin finely toothed. Upper surface is a deep sub-shiny green; underside woolly and pale shiny green, with five to six raised veins. Leaf stalk 2.5–5 cm.

Use
Fill a small jar with ripe berries, add plenty of sugar and top up with brandy. Save as a treat to top off the Christmas pudding instead of inedible holly.

White flowers, 1.5 cm across, with 5 spreading petals, in clusters 5–12 cm across. Twenty stamens and two styles, opening in June and strongly (to some, unpleasantly) scented.

Shoot green and woolly when new, becoming hairless and shiny brown. Buds globe or egg shaped, 0.4–0.6 cm, shiny green, with brown hairs at the tips.

Deciduous tree

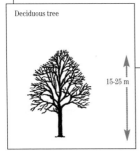

15-25 m

The Wild Service Tree is rather different from any other tree in the genus Sorbus, with its large, pointed-lobed leaves, which become attractively mottled with russet at the end of the year. The large summer clusters of white flowers are followed in autumn by small, hard berries. They are greenish-brown and covered with small dots, giving the impression of tiny pears. They are also very bitter at first, but become edible and sweet when they have started to rot on the tree, or 'blet'. This happens in mid- to late autumn, which is when they should be gathered, or immediately after the first frost.

COOKING AND EATING The berries can be used like Rowan berries for making jelly, or even eaten simply with cream and sugar, as the seeds are very small. They also make a surprisingly good light fruit cake. Cream 125 g butter with 125 g caster sugar to a smooth consistency. Gradually mix in 2 eggs and 250 g self-raising flour. Add about 90 ml milk, a little mixed spice and 125 g Wild Service berries, making sure that they are soft and ripe and any little stalks are removed. Transfer to a greased and lined 18 cm cake tin and bake for 50–60 minutes at 180°C, or until well risen and golden brown. The berries give the cake a sweet but sharp lemony taste, perfect with a glass of port.

The Wild Service Tree is an occasional tree of woods and hedgerows, but rarely occurs in any great numbers. The crown becomes domed in old trees.

BARK
Smooth dark brown or grey on young trees. As the tree matures, it develops fissures and shallow, scaly plates.

Rowan

Rowan

Sorbus aucuparia

Use

For a pink gin, squeeze fresh Rowan berry juice into a glass over ice cubes; swirl around to cool and coat the glass with the juice, then throw out the ice. Pour in a measure of gin, add a lemon twist and drink neat.

Fruit ripens from August, turning from green through orange to scarlet. It is pumpkin-shaped, 0.6–0.9 cm.

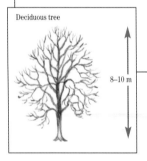

Deciduous tree

8–10 m

Flowers in large clusters on the ends of the shoots in late spring. They are 10—15 cm across, and composed of many small creamy-white flowers, which smell unpleasant to some people.

Pinnate leaves (divided into leaflets) alternate on the shoot, up to 20 cm by 12 cm; 13 to 15 leaflets,. 3-7 cm by 1.5-2.3 cm, an oblong egg shape. They are set directly on the central stalk, except for the end leaflet. Margin has coarse teeth. Upper surface matt green, lower surface light green and generally with white hairs.

Shoot green, with sparse white hairs at first; grey brown in second year. Buds (1–1.7 cm), egg to cone shaped, with white hairs.

Rowan is native throughout Europe, and twice a year makes an extremely attractive tree. First, in early summer, when it is covered with domed clusters of creamy flowers, which look wonderful, but smell dreadful, and then again in early autumn, when the flowers are replaced by bunches of orange-scarlet berries. It is fairly common in the wild, preferring sandy or acid soils, and is often found growing with birch trees, even in mountains, up to the treeline. It is also planted as an ornamental in streets and gardens.

COOKING AND EATING The fruits are quite bitter and need to be picked as soon as they are ripe or the birds will have them all. This rather tart jelly is the perfect accompaniment to strongly flavoured game dishes such as pheasant or venison, but it may be made milder by replacing half the berries with cooking or Crab Apples, or more tangy by adding a tablespoon of chopped Thyme leaves. Gently simmer 1 kg washed berries in 350ml water until soft, squashing them from time to time to extract the juice. Strain through a jelly bag. Measure the juice and add 450 g sugar to each 600 ml of juice; warm until dissolved, then boil for 10 minutes or until setting point is reached. See page 20 for more detail on making fruit jellies.

Rowan is characteristic of moorland, but also occurs in lowland broadleaved and conifer forest. It has an upright, rather conical habit, but older trees are more rounded.

BARK
Smooth shiny grey or silvery grey, becoming browner on old trees and forming scaly ridges at the base.

Sloe

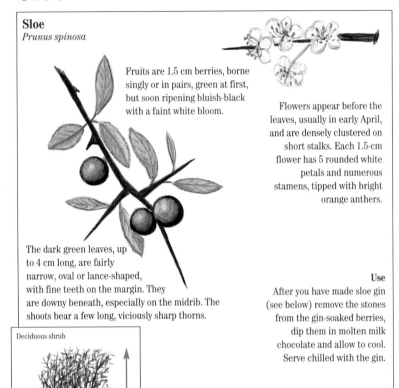

Sloe
Prunus spinosa

Fruits are 1.5 cm berries, borne singly or in pairs, green at first, but soon ripening bluish-black with a faint white bloom.

Flowers appear before the leaves, usually in early April, and are densely clustered on short stalks. Each 1.5-cm flower has 5 rounded white petals and numerous stamens, tipped with bright orange anthers.

The dark green leaves, up to 4 cm long, are fairly narrow, oval or lance-shaped, with fine teeth on the margin. They are downy beneath, especially on the midrib. The shoots bear a few long, viciously sharp thorns.

Deciduous shrub

5m

Use
After you have made sloe gin (see below) remove the stones from the gin-soaked berries, dip them in molten milk chocolate and allow to cool. Serve chilled with the gin.

Sloe, or Blackthorn as it is also known, bursts into life in early spring with a dazzling display of flowers. It occurs in thickets as a shrub up to 5 m high, usually in dampish spots or along the margins of ditches. The leaves start to appear just as the flowers are fading, and the shrub sinks back into obscurity again for a few months until the magnificent fruits ripen in early autumn.

COOKING AND EATING The fruits in their natural state are incredibly sour and quite inedible, but famously are used to make the delicious, and fiercely potent, Sloe gin. Take 200 g Sloe berries and pierce the skin or slit it with a knife. If the berries have been subject to frost, this won't be necessary (putting them in the freezer for 24 hours will also split the skin). Put them into a large jar and add 125 g caster sugar, then top up with a 750 ml bottle of gin. Keep it for at least three months, giving the jar an occasional stir, and it should be ready in time for Christmas.

The gin will gradually turn a sumptuous shade of pinkish-purple. A cinnamon stick will add extra flavour, if desired, and some suggest the inclusion of cloves, but they can become overpowering. Strain the gin before bottling it, and serve in a shot glass.

Sloe occurs as clumps, thickets or hedgerows up to 5 m high. It spreads by means of suckers and can be very invasive, so tends to form an untidy tangle that is rather unattractive in winter.

BARK
Generally fairly smooth, dark grey-black in colour. Rarely forming cracks or fissures, since the trunks do not become very large.

Crab Apple

Crab Apple
Malus sylvestris

Leaves alternate on the shoot, 3-7 cm by 2-4 cm, oval to egg shaped, tapering to the acute tip and rounded or wedge shaped at the base. Margins have fine, rounded teeth. Upper surface dark glossy green, uderside paler, generally with few or no hairs. Stalk 2-3 cm long.

Shoots are grey brown, with dark brown, egg-shaped to cone-shaped buds.

Deciduous tree

10-15 m

Tip
Wild Crab Apples are rarely planted, but ornamental varieties with brightly coloured fruits are often seen in streets, parks and gardens. Their fruit may also be used for making jellies and jams.

White or pink flowers in clusters of four to seven, appearing with the new leaves.

Spur shoots may end in a thorn.

Fruit (2-3 cm by 2-4 cm). globe shaped, or wider than long, indented at both ends. It is green and russet and carries persistent remains of the old flower,

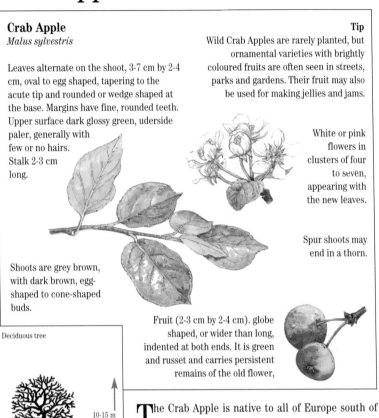

The Crab Apple is native to all of Europe south of around 60 degrees north, but absent from Portugal and adjacent regions of Spain. It is often a difficult tree to spot when growing in a mixed hedgerow or in broadleaved woodland, for it is often quite tall – so the flowers are out of sight. In the autumn, however, huge quantities of fruit scattered over the woodland floor or roadside betray its presence. The fruit has a rubbery texture and a sour taste, and can not be eaten fresh, but they do contain plenty of pectin and are therefore very useful for making jams and jellies. Sometimes, Crab Apples that have hybridized with domestic varieties produce small trees, with sharp, but edible, fruits.

Cooking and eating Crab Apple jelly is excellent on its own, but is also a superb base for a variety of jellies flavoured with wild fruits or herbs. Natural partners include Cranberries, Elderberries, Elder flowers, Sloes, Mint, Rosemary or Thyme. Crab Apples are easy to prepare since they need not be peeled or cored, just roughly chopped. Following the recipe on page 20, using enough water to just cover the fruit, and simmer gently in a covered pan until soft, mashing the fruit from time to time to extract more juice. After straining, use 450 g of sugar to each 600 ml of juice extracted.

Crab Apple develops a domed, leafy crown, rounded in old trees but more conical and spiky in young ones. *Malus domestica*, the Orchard Apple, has much bigger fruit and is hairy in all its parts.

BARK
Smooth and green brown with large orange breathing pores (lenticels) in young trees, becoming brown and cracked in old trees.

Elderberry

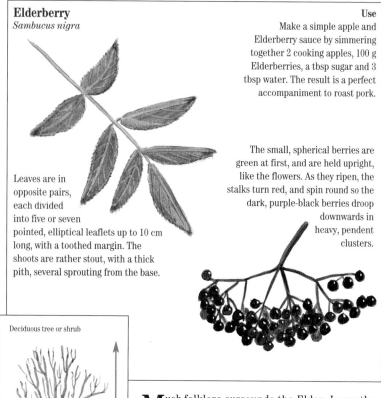

Elderberry
Sambucus nigra

Use
Make a simple apple and Elderberry sauce by simmering together 2 cooking apples, 100 g Elderberries, a tbsp sugar and 3 tbsp water. The result is a perfect accompaniment to roast pork.

The small, spherical berries are green at first, and are held upright, like the flowers. As they ripen, the stalks turn red, and spin round so the dark, purple-black berries droop downwards in heavy, pendent clusters.

Leaves are in opposite pairs, each divided into five or seven pointed, elliptical leaflets up to 10 cm long, with a toothed margin. The shoots are rather stout, with a thick pith, several sprouting from the base.

Deciduous tree or shrub

4-8 m

Much folklore surrounds the Elder. In northern Europe there is a widespread belief that it is bad luck to burn its wood, and that it may act as a protection against witches. The berries are usually as abundant as the flowers (which I treat separately on page 74), and shrubs may be festooned with the heavy, wine-black fruits in late summer or autumn. They must be gathered as soon as they start dropping and turn from deep red to black. They have a deep, claret-like flavour, a little too sharp to eat raw but perfectly good cooked with sugar.

COOKING AND EATING Elderberries make excellent wine, or a superb jam if mixed with an equal weight of Blackberries. Or try this chutney, which complements strong cheeses. Combine 500 g each of Elderberries, onions and cooking apples in a large pan with 250 ml of malt or red wine vinegar, and a tsp each of mixed spice, cayenne pepper and salt. Bring to the boil and simmer for 30 minutes, then add another 200 ml vinegar and 350 g granulated sugar. Stir until dissolved, then simmer for a further 30 minutes until thick. Keep in sterilized jars for at least two months before eating.

170

Elder grows as a small tree or, more commonly, a large shrub, often rather straggly with arching stems. It is often heavily-laden with dark purple berries in early autumn. It grows throughout Europe except northern Scandinavia, and flowers in June and July.

BARK
Grey-brown, with deep furrows and a corky texture. Often colonised by Jew's Ear fungus (page 216).

Dog Rose

Dog Rose
Rosa canina

Uses
Rose hips may be combined with apples to make a richly coloured jelly, and a tea can be made from the leaves. Dog Rose is unsuitable for rose water; instead use the petals of deep red, scented, garden varieties.

The hips are oval or flask-shaped, ripening to a bright, shiny red.

The flowers are usually pink, and about 50 mm across. They have five notched petals and many yellow stamens. The styles in the centre of the flower form a tiny rounded dome.

Leaves are divided into (usually) five well-separated leaflets, each with a finely toothed edge.

Hedgerows

Nothing is more suggestive of the summer than a roadside hedge covered with roses. Dog Rose produces its flowers in early summer and usually has pink petals, or white petals flushed with pink. The hips are ripe at the end of summer when the blackberries are ready. The familiar rose hip is actually a swelling of that part of the stem that holds the flower; the true fruits are the hairy objects within, each containing one seed.

COOKING AND EATING Syrup made from the hips contains large amounts of vitamin C and has been vitally important for public health in the past when other fresh fruits were not available. To make the syrup, wash and chop 500g of hips and simmer them in 1 litre of water for 5 minutes only. Leave them to stand, covered, for a further 15 minutes, to extract more of the flavour. Strain the liquid, and for every two cups of liquid add one cup of sugar. Heat again until just dissolved, but do not cook for longer as this destroys the vitamin C. The syrup, when cool, can be diluted to taste, or a spoonful can be taken a day to keep colds at bay. It is very good dribbled over vanilla ice cream. Keep the syrup in the fridge, or freeze it into cubes to use when needed.

Dog Rose *is a bushy plant, with large thorns, which produces an abundance of flowers, usually of the most delightful shade of pink. It may form free-standing bushes, or trail over other hedgerow plants, sometimes to a considerable height. The flowering period is short, but in early autumn the branches bear a crop of bright red fruits.*

Dog Rose

RANGE: Throughout Europe, except the far north.

HABITAT: Hedgerows, scrub and woodland margins.

FLOWERING TIME: Flowers from June to July.
Fruits from August to September.

173

Blackberry

Blackberry
Rubus fruticosus

Use
Blackberries make excellent jam and are a perfect mixer for more acidic fruits such as Elderberries or Crab Apples. They are even better made into a jelly since there are no pips.

Each leaf is divided into three separate, rather broad leaflets, sometimes with fine prickles on the veins underneath.

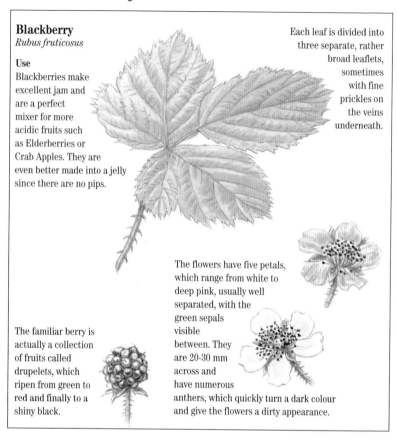

The familiar berry is actually a collection of fruits called drupelets, which ripen from green to red and finally to a shiny black.

The flowers have five petals, which range from white to deep pink, usually well separated, with the green sepals visible between. They are 20-30 mm across and have numerous anthers, which quickly turn a dark colour and give the flowers a dirty appearance.

Hedgerows, roadsides

Blackberry, or Bramble, is surely one of the most successful of plants. It can cope with a huge variety of habitats on a wide range of soils, and seems to be equally at home on the harsh, dry sands of a dune system as it is on the rich humus of sheltered woodland. It can be found in almost any habitat, but particularly on wasteground and in hedgerows and woods, avoiding very wet soils. The fruits are available from late summer onwards, and the biggest and best ones are usually the first to ripen at the tips of the stems. Thereafter, the fruits become progressively smaller and sharper.

COOKING AND EATING Blackberries are perhaps the most bounteous of edible wild fruits and it makes sense to make as much use of them as possible. They can be preserved easily by freezing on an open tray and then bagging them up when they are frozen. The classic autumn dish is apple and blackberry pie. Peel and core 500 g cooking apples, slice them and cook gently with 100 g sugar and a tablespoon of water until they are just beginning to soften. Add 250 g of washed Blackberries and continue cooking for a minute or two, then check for sweetness. Put the mixture into a dish lined with shortcrust pastry, seal with a pastry lid and bake until the pastry is lightly browned. Serve with ice cream.

Blackberry is an extremely variable plant, but is hard to miss as the thorns so readily attach themselves to clothing, or even bare skin. The flowers, often in profusion, although similar, always appear grubbier and less tidy than those of the roses which have larger, neater flowers. The edible fruits, which may appear at the same time as the flowers, are unmistakeable.

Blackberry

RANGE: Throughout Europe, except the far north.

HABITAT: Almost anywhere, but particularly waste ground, hedgerows and woods, avoiding very wet soils.

FLOWERING TIME: May to November.
FRUIT: August to October.

175

Dewberry

Dewberry
Rubus caesius

Tip
The drupelets of Dewberry are very squashy and held tightly by the calyx of sepals beneath them, so it is better to snip off the fruits with their stalks using scissors, and remove the fruit more carefully later.

Flowers are almost always white, like a rose's, with five petals and numerous stamens.

Leaves are almost identical to those of Blackberry, with three coarsely toothed leaflets, and a whitish bloom on the younger shoots. But the stems have smaller, weaker prickles.

The fruit is like a small, deformed Blackberry, with fewer drupelets (sometimes only three), often in various sizes clustered together, and with a greyish bloom over the blue-black surface.

Grassland, scrub

Dewberry is in some senses the poor country cousin of the Blackberry (page 174), for it is a slighter plant with weaker prickles and curious fruits that look as though they have not formed properly. It grows in rough grassland or among scrub, usually over limestone soils, and is often, though by no means exclusively, found near the sea. The infused leaves make an excellent tea. The berries take a little more searching out than those of Blackberry, but they are worth the trouble because their flavour is more subtle. However, Dewberries rarely become very sweet.

Cooking and eating To make a Dewberry sorbet, add 150 g of granulated sugar to 300 ml of water, heating until the sugar dissolves. Bring to the boil and continue to heat for five minutes until it turns to syrup, then leave to cool. Put 500 g of Dewberries into a pan and heat gently until they soften, then pass them through a sieve and stir in to the syrup. Put the mixture into the freezer for a few minutes, and whisk two egg whites until stiff. When the dewberry mixture has frozen enough to become slushy, whisk it to break up any ice crystals and gently fold in the egg white. Freeze again until firm. Use a heated spoon to remove portions, and serve with mint leaves and Dewberry fruits.

Dewberry *is an untidy and sprawling, shrubby plant, generally growing to knee- or waist-height, though in grazed areas it may creep along the ground. It has a weaker, more fragile appearance than its close relative the Blackberry, but the smaller fruits have a finer flavour.*

Dewberry

RANGE: Throughout Europe except northern Scandinavia and Scotland.

HABITAT: Rough grasslands or scrub, often near the sea.

FLOWERING TIME: May to September.

Cloudberry

Cloudberry
Rubus chamaemorus

Use
Make a traditional, quick dessert by whipping 1 cup of cream with 2 tbsp of sugar with a drop of vanilla essence, and gently folding in whole, ripe Cloudberries.

Rather rough and leathery leaves with a crinkled surface, more or less kidney-shaped in outline with three to five lobes and a coarsely toothed margin.

The flowers are 15-20 mm across, and have five rounded white petals which are well separated so that the sepals show between them. Male and female flowers are on separate plants, the male sporting numerous yellow stamens.

The highly distinctive fruit is a collection of up to 20 little balls or 'drupelets' like a Blackberry, but which ripen to a bright orange colour, held upright on a short stalk just above the leaves.

Heathland

Cloudberry is well adapted to the harsh conditions of the Arctic tundra, although it also occurs on heaths and moors. In order to keep out of the wind, it rarely grows more than 20 cm high, and the rough, hairy leaves help to prevent it from drying out. Each plant only produces one flower, and therefore potentially only one fruit. Many plants produce no flowers at all, so fruit is never produced in great abundance. The fruits contain a large amount of vitamin C, and are highly sought after as they stay fresh for a long time, and may be frozen or used in preserves. People have tried to grow Cloudberry as a crop in an attempt to overcome the low and unpredictable productivity it has in the wild.

COOKING AND EATING Jam may be made by using exactly the same technique as for Blackberry (page 174), using equal quantities of fruit and sugar. Cloudberry jam has a distinctive taste, much prized in Scandinavia, and is best without the addition of other fruit. Spread creamy blue cheese on to crisp bread and place a small spoonful of cloudberry jam on top: quite a delicacy. For effect, decorate a tray of these snacks with bright blue borage flowers.

Cloudberry *hugs and covers the ground like patches of carpet, so that the landscape is punctuated with white flowers in summer and dotted with tiny orange 'lollipops' of fruit in early autumn. The fruits are more difficult to spot in the south of its range, where plants are less bountiful.*

Cloudberry

RANGE: Throughout Scandinavia. Occurs in northern England and Scotland, but rare.

HABITAT: Heaths and moors.

FLOWERING TIME: June to August.

Fennel

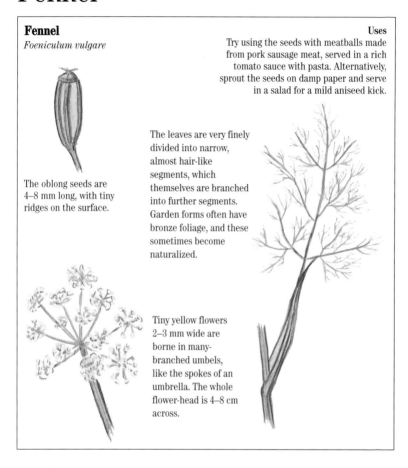

Fennel

Foeniculum vulgare

Uses

Try using the seeds with meatballs made from pork sausage meat, served in a rich tomato sauce with pasta. Alternatively, sprout the seeds on damp paper and serve in a salad for a mild aniseed kick.

The oblong seeds are 4–8 mm long, with tiny ridges on the surface.

The leaves are very finely divided into narrow, almost hair-like segments, which themselves are branched into further segments. Garden forms often have bronze foliage, and these sometimes become naturalized.

Tiny yellow flowers 2–3 mm wide are borne in many-branched umbels, like the spokes of an umbrella. The whole flower-head is 4–8 cm across.

Wasteland, roadsides

The stature of this tall and rather elegant plant makes it recognisable even at a distance. It grows singly or in small patches on roadsides, wasteland and in rocky places, usually on chalky soils and often close to the sea. The plant has a long history of medicinal use, especially for treating indigestion, and a herbal tea made either with the leaves or the seeds is a useful remedy. The fennel bulb sold as a vegetable is the variety *azoricum*, or Florence Fennel, which has swollen leaf bases, and is found only in cultivation.

COOKING AND EATING The seeds have a sweeter flavour than the leaves; both have a sweet aniseed element and a bitter element, but are sweeter if grown in a warm climate and well dried before use. Fresh leaves make superb stuffing for whole fish such as sea bass. They can also be used to flavour sauces such as this *buerre blanc*. Finely chop a shallot and add it to 1 tablespoon of white wine vinegar and the juice of a lemon. Throw in 2 or 3 roughly chopped Fennel leaves and boil the stock until it is reduced by half. Over a low heat, gradually whisk in 50 g butter until the sauce is light and frothy. Season with salt and pepper and serve over delicate fish such as turbot, plaice or sole.

Fennel *grows to shoulder-height or more, usually as scattered plants by the roadside. It has a rather stately but delicate appearance, often growing much taller than the surrounding vegetation, and is easily recognised by the feathery leaves and numerous umbels of yellow flowers.*

Fennel

RANGE: Coastal areas of southern Britain, Western France and the Mediterranean region, sometimes inland.

HABITAT: Roadsides, wasteland, on chalky soil.

FLOWERING TIME: June to October.

181

Cauliflower Fungus

Cauliflower Fungus
Sparassis crispa

Collecting
The Cauliflower Fungus often reappears in the same place year after year. Rather than remove the whole fruiting body, cut away half, leaving the rest in the ground to produce spores for future generations.

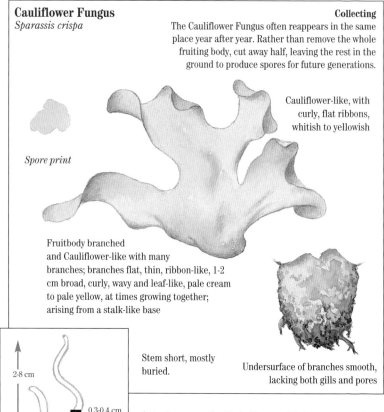

Cauliflower-like, with curly, flat ribbons, whitish to yellowish

Spore print

Fruitbody branched and Cauliflower-like with many branches; branches flat, thin, ribbon-like, 1-2 cm broad, curly, wavy and leaf-like, pale cream to pale yellow, at times growing together; arising from a stalk-like base

2-8 cm

0.3-0.4 cm

Stem short, mostly buried.

Undersurface of branches smooth, lacking both gills and pores

Also known as the Brain Fungus, this is a root parasite of pine trees, growing on stumps or nearby. The fruitbodies can reach 40 cm across, and may weigh between 1 and 5 kg, though record specimens have been measured at 14 kg. The fungus makes good eating and dries well – it is a shame that it is not more common. The convoluted folds produce spores on one surface only, and have a soft, rubbery texture. Their one drawback is that the numerous nooks and crannies within them make excellent hiding places for small insects. As these insects grow, they tend to draw up pine needles with them that become enveloped within the flesh: a good deal of careful cleaning is necessary. They have a mild but very pleasant taste, and a curious ammonia-like smell when fresh, though this disappears after brief cooking. Avoid older specimens that have begun to dry and develop crispy margins to the folds.

Cooking and eating They are excellent if fried briefly in butter, added to a cream sauce and served with green spinach pasta, or black sepia pasta that is coloured with cuttlefish ink (available from delicatessen stores). Alternatively, break some into large chunks and dust with flour, before frying for a few minutes in butter with some sliced red peppers. Add a small quantity of chicken stock and white wine, and reduce it down to a thick sauce, seasoning with black pepper and parsley.

182

Habitat: *On stumps and at base of conifers, especially pine.*

LOOKALIKES

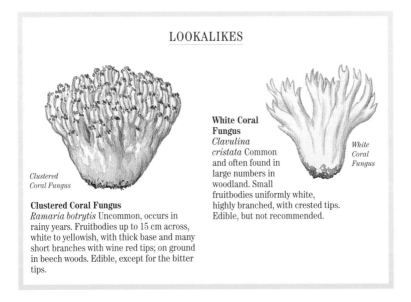

*Clustered
Coral Fungus*

Clustered Coral Fungus
Ramaria botrytis Uncommon, occurs in
rainy years. Fruitbodies up to 15 cm across,
white to yellowish, with thick base and many
short branches with wine red tips; on ground
in beech woods. Edible, except for the bitter
tips.

**White Coral
Fungus**
*Clavulina
cristata* Common
and often found in
large numbers in
woodland. Small
fruitbodies uniformly white,
highly branched, with crested tips.
Edible, but not recommended.

*White
Coral
Fungus*

Horn of Plenty

Horn of Plenty
Craterellus cornucopioides

Tip
It is difficult to spot these dark mushrooms in the leaf litter, but once the eye has been trained by finding the first, there should be plenty of others nearby.

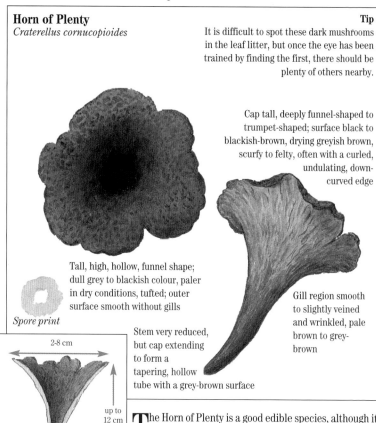

Cap tall, deeply funnel-shaped to trumpet-shaped; surface black to blackish-brown, drying greyish brown, scurfy to felty, often with a curled, undulating, down-curved edge

Tall, high, hollow, funnel shape; dull grey to blackish colour, paler in dry conditions, tufted; outer surface smooth without gills

Spore print

Gill region smooth to slightly veined and wrinkled, pale brown to grey-brown

Stem very reduced, but cap extending to form a tapering, hollow tube with a grey-brown surface

2-8 cm

up to 12 cm

The Horn of Plenty is a good edible species, although its dark colour has earned it the rather sinister names of *'trompettes des morts'* (trumpet of the dead) and 'black trumpet'. In France, it is known as *'la viande des pauvres'* (poor man's meat). It is distinctly vase- or trumpet-shaped and hollow, with very little true stem, and the lower, solid part should be discarded before cooking. It has a firm texture and dries well, so is very suitable for use in stews and soups. It also has a very good flavour, so doesn't require much seasoning.

COOKING AND EATING For a rich Horn of Plenty Strogonoff, take some fillet steak and cut it into strips about 2 cm wide. Do the same with a generous handful of Horn of Plenty mushrooms. Using a deep frying pan, fry them both in butter, adding some chopped garlic, until the steak is well browned but not overdone – it should still have some 'give'. Remove the mushrooms and meat, and deglaze the pan with a small glass of red wine, boiling it until the wine is reduced by two-thirds. Then add half to 1 cup of sour cream, and again reduce it a little before returning the mushrooms and the meat to the pan, and seasoning with salt, black pepper and parsley. Serve with mashed potatoes or rice.

Habitat: *Clustered, in both deciduous and coniferous woodland, but especially common in woodlands of hazel, beech and oak; also grows in mossy pine woods.*

LOOKALIKES

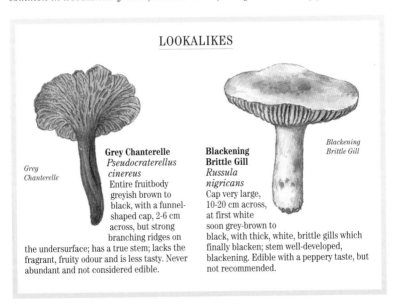

Grey Chanterelle

Grey Chanterelle
Pseudocraterellus cinereus
Entire fruitbody greyish brown to black, with a funnel-shaped cap, 2-6 cm across, but strong branching ridges on the undersurface; has a true stem; lacks the fragrant, fruity odour and is less tasty. Never abundant and not considered edible.

Blackening Brittle Gill

Blackening Brittle Gill
Russula nigricans
Cap very large, 10-20 cm across, at first white soon grey-brown to black, with thick, white, brittle gills which finally blacken; stem well-developed, blackening. Edible with a peppery taste, but not recommended.

Hedgehog Fungus

Hedgehog Fungus
Hydnum repandum

Tip
Older specimens of Hedgehog Fungus can be bitter, and some recommend that the mushroom is blanched before cooking or that the spines are removed, though they tend to break off anyway.

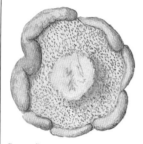

Fruitbody firm fleshy, whitish to pinkish buff; lower surface covered with numerous, fine spines, short stocky stem

Cap at first convex, variable, cushion-shaped to depressed; surface white to pale pinkish buff, velvety to felty becoming smooth and shiny when dry, not zoned; margin entire, thick, persistently inrolled

Spines adnate, at times subdecurrent at least down one side of the stem, white or with a pinkish tint; individual spines soft and brittle, fragile, uneven in length, 4-8 mm long, very crowded

Stem central but mostly excentric, fairly stocky, cylindrical or swollen below; solid; surface whitish, paler than pileus, covered with fine hairs, becoming smooth, arising from a mass of fungal threads

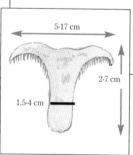

5-17 cm

2-7 cm

1.5-4 cm

Occuring alone or in small groups, Hedgehog Fungus is not likely to be confused with other mushrooms. The pale colour and the little, soft spines under the cap in place of gills are very useful distinguishing features. Usually sold under the French name *'pied de mouton'* (sheep's foot), it is a firm, fleshy species that makes good eating. Occasionally, a pure white form is found, which tends to be more robust and firmer in texture. Young, fresh specimens are not bitter, but the firm texture demands that Hedgehog Fungus is always well cooked – it works particularly well in stews.

COOKING AND EATING Hedgehog Fungus has a delicate flavour all its own, which can be best appreciated in the following simple pasta dish. First, put some pasta in boiling water; a robust, firm variety such as *penne* or *conchiglie* is best. In a separate pan, gently fry some sliced Hedgehog Fungi, including the stems, in olive oil. Drain off any water and continue to cook on a low heat, adding some finely sliced garlic, for a further five minutes. Add a generous splash of dry sherry and some chopped Wild Marjoram or Thyme, and allow to reduce by half. Then add about half a cup of single cream, and continue with the reduction, seasoning with salt and pepper. When the sauce has thickened a little, throw in some fresh, chopped parsley and mix with the drained pasta.

Habitat: *Amongst humus in deciduous woods, especially oak, beech and birch where it can be abundant, but also found in pine and spruce woodland.*

LOOKALIKES

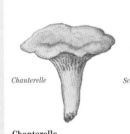

Chanterelle

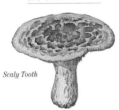

Scaly Tooth

Scaly Tooth
Sarcodon imbricatus Easily distinguished by the yellowish brown cap with rings of coarse scales. Thick stem is brownish and the spines soon become brown. Widespread but rare, in coniferous woods. Inedible and worthless.

Chanterelle
Cantharellus cibarius
Although differing in structure, this is closely related and superficially similar to the Wood Urchin.

Strongly-scented Spine Fungus
Phellodon confluens Caps normally fusing to form compound fruitbodies, at first white becoming brownish, with pale greyish spines. On the ground in leafy woods, such as beech, chestnut and oak. Widespread but uncommon. Inedible.

Strongly-scented Spine Fungus

Field Blewit

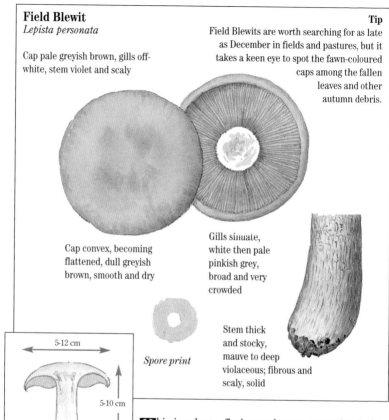

Field Blewit
Lepista personata

Cap pale greyish brown, gills off-white, stem violet and scaly

Tip
Field Blewits are worth searching for as late as December in fields and pastures, but it takes a keen eye to spot the fawn-coloured caps among the fallen leaves and other autumn debris.

Cap convex, becoming flattened, dull greyish brown, smooth and dry

Gills sinuate, white then pale pinkish grey, broad and very crowded

Spore print

Stem thick and stocky, mauve to deep violaceous; fibrous and scaly, solid

5-12 cm

5-10 cm

1-2 cm

This is a large, fleshy mushroom, appearing in late autumn and early winter. It is easily identified by the mauve-coloured stem and pinkish gills, and is sometimes known as 'blue-legs'. It has a close relative in the slightly more common Wood Blewit, which has a darker cap and stunning violet gills. Both are edible after cooking, but the Field Blewit is reckoned to have the finer flavour. They have an aromatic flavour and are inclined to become a little soft on cooking, but they should still be cooked thoroughly.

COOKING AND EATING They work well mixed with other mushrooms in pies or stews, but are good on their own in this pancake: sauté sliced blewits in butter with garlic over a high heat until they start to brown. Then add a little cream, parsley, salt and pepper and continue cooking to reduce the sauce until thick. Prepare some pancakes by making a batter using 100 g plain flour, 200 ml milk, 1 egg and a pinch of salt. Whisk really well, and cook the pancakes in a very hot, slightly oiled pan. Spread the mushroom mixture on to a pancake and roll it up. If you use clingfilm, then the pancake can be rolled tightly, without squeezing out the filling. Remove the clingfilm and pop the pancakes under the grill to warm through before serving.

Habitat: *In grassland, often at edge of woods.*

LOOKALIKES

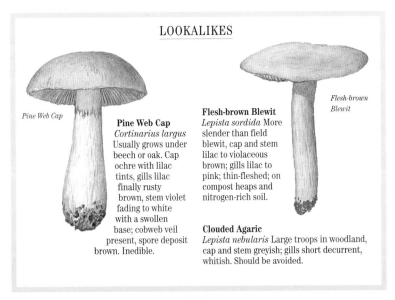

Pine Web Cap

Pine Web Cap
Cortinarius largus
Usually grows under beech or oak. Cap ochre with lilac tints, gills lilac finally rusty brown, stem violet fading to white with a swollen base; cobweb veil present, spore deposit brown. Inedible.

Flesh-brown Blewit
Lepista sordida More slender than field blewit, cap and stem lilac to violaceous brown; gills lilac to pink; thin-fleshed; on compost heaps and nitrogen-rich soil.

Flesh-brown Blewit

Clouded Agaric
Lepista nebularis Large troops in woodland, cap and stem greyish; gills short decurrent, whitish. Should be avoided.

Honey Fungus

Honey Fungus
Armillaria mellea

Dense clusters at tree bases;
yellow-brown caps, pale
decurrent gills, large ring on
stem; black threads under bark

Tip
Always cook very
thoroughly, and try just a
small amount if eating
for the first time.

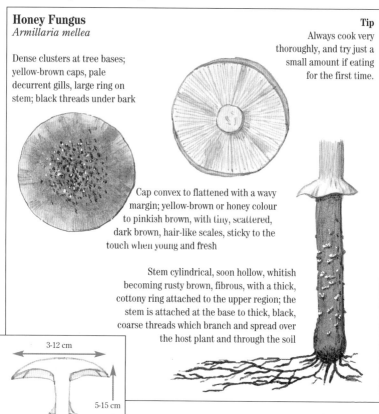

Cap convex to flattened with a wavy
margin; yellow-brown or honey colour
to pinkish brown, with tiny, scattered,
dark brown, hair-like scales, sticky to the
touch when young and fresh

Stem cylindrical, soon hollow, whitish
becoming rusty brown, fibrous, with a thick,
cottony ring attached to the upper region; the
stem is attached at the base to thick, black,
coarse threads which branch and spread over
the host plant and through the soil

3-12 cm

5-15 cm

1-2 cm

A common, fleshy mushroom, Honey Fungus grows in large tufts on stumps and among tree roots in late autumn, often very abundantly. It is variable in colour and in the extent of scales on the cap and stem, and recently it has been split into several new species based on these differences, but we are dealing here with *Armillaria mellea* in the wide sense. It is a major problem for forestry, as it attacks trees and shrubs, causing severe damage. Underneath the bark of the tree you can usually find a network of flattened, black strands formed from the mycelium; these explain the alternative name of 'boot-lace fungus'. Although this species is frequently eaten, some care needs to be taken as it can cause gastric upsets in some people, and should never be eaten raw. Only young specimens should be eaten; the older ones have a bitter taste and contain more toxin.

COOKING AND EATING Some recommend that they should be blanched in boiling water for a few minutes, discarding this water before cooking, though this does tend to remove any flavour altogether, which can be described as mild at best. However, the texture remains firm even after cooking, and it is not unpleasant if well fried with some strong flavours such as onion and garlic, and then added to an omelette.

Habitat: *Clustered on roots and stumps of many deciduous trees.*

LOOKALIKES

Ringless Honey Fungus
Armillaria tabescens Very similar but the cap is dry and the stem lacks a ring. Cap yellowish brown to tawny brown, with small, rusty brown scales of fine fibres towards disk; stem tapering below, whitish, bruising brown; usually found on wood of deciduous trees; western Europe but not in Scandinavia.

Sulphur Tuft
Hypholoma fasciculare Fruitbody uniformly sulphur yellow, but adnate gills finally purplish black. Stem yellowish, with a ring-like zone of dark brown fibres. Can cause severe gastric upsets.

Two-toned Scale Head
Kuehneromyces mutabilis Clustered on old stumps and dead tree bases throughout summer and autumn. Recognized by the brown, two-tone cap (above) and dark brown, scaly stem (right) with a small ring.

Two-toned Scale Head

Beefsteak Fungus

Beefsteak Fungus
Fistulina hepatica

Reddish brown fleshy bracket, at base of oak or chestnut trunk; separate tubes in tube layer

Use

This love-it-or-loathe-it fungus can be coated in egg and breadcrumbs flavoured with garlic and chilli, before frying in hot oil.

Spore print

Cap bracket-shaped to tongue-like, with a pinkish to orange-red surface, sticky and finely warty

Stem absent, the cap tapering laterally to a thick point of attachment

Tube layer up to 1 cm deep, individual tubes separated from each other, opening by tiny pores, 2-3 per mm, at first whitish then yellowish, bruising reddish brown

7-20 cm

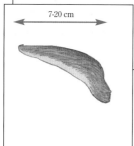

This is a peculiar fungus: it belongs to a family of its own and is unlikely to be confused with any others. It is generally grouped among the 'polypores' because of its fine, vertical tubes under the cap. However, on the Beefsteak these tubes are separated from each other, and represent elongations of minute, inverted cups. The fungus is unpopular in forestry as it causes a brownish coloured rot, which stains surrounding wood. Such 'brown oak' is, however, sought after among furniture makers. It is also known as 'oak-' or 'ox-tongue' fungus, and has the curious appearance and texture of raw steak – it even exudes a red juice, like watery blood. It contains a high proportion of tannic acid which it extracts from its host tree, resulting in a sour flavour. Considered by some to make an excellent, even five-star dish, others, including this author, find it thoroughly disappointing. It may be that specimens growing on Sweet Chestnut have less tannic acid than those on Oak.

COOKING AND EATING Some recommend that the fungus should be parboiled several times, discarding the water to remove the acid. The fans, however, cook it in a little water with butter, garlic, salt, pepper and herbs for 10 minutes, reducing the stock to a sauce. Be prepared for the brilliant, meaty red colour to wash out to an unappetising grey.

Habitat: *Singly on lower branches and stumps of old Oak and Sweet Chestnut trees.*

LOOKALIKES

There are no close relatives or lookalikes to this fungus. Although apparently similar to the bracket-like polypores, its affinity lies with a dissimilar group, known as the *cyphellas*. If the lower pore surface is closely examined, it will be seen that the many and crowded vertical tubes grow separately from each other, not fused together. It is only found on large and old trees, and is the main cause of decay of oak tree trunks, making them hollow.

Parasol Mushroom

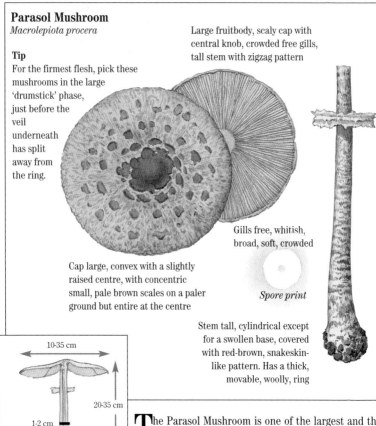

Parasol Mushroom
Macrolepiota procera

Tip
For the firmest flesh, pick these mushrooms in the large 'drumstick' phase, just before the veil underneath has split away from the ring.

Large fruitbody, scaly cap with central knob, crowded free gills, tall stem with zigzag pattern

Gills free, whitish, broad, soft, crowded

Cap large, convex with a slightly raised centre, with concentric small, pale brown scales on a paler ground but entire at the centre

Spore print

Stem tall, cylindrical except for a swollen base, covered with red-brown, snakeskin-like pattern. Has a thick, movable, woolly, ring

10-35 cm

20-35 cm

1-2 cm

The Parasol Mushroom is one of the largest and the best of the European edible mushrooms. Where they occur they may be found in some numbers and go on fruiting for several weeks. It is often confused with the Shaggy Parasol but the tall, scaly stem and the non-reddening flesh will readily identify the Parasol proper. Young fruit bodies resemble drumsticks, with the fully formed stem bearing a knob-like, unopened cap.

COOKING AND EATING They are best eaten before the caps have fully opened out, when the flesh can lose some of its firmness. This recipe makes use of the ready-made cup provided by young specimens. Chop up a small quantity of field or other edible mushrooms (you could use the cap of a fully opened Parasol or shop-bought button mushrooms, at a pinch) and fry in butter together with chopped bacon and garlic. Discard the stem of the Parasol – they are always too tough and fibrous to use, and place a small knob of butter in the cap. Mix the fried mushrooms and bacon with a little beaten egg and a handful of breadcrumbs, and season. Fill up the Parasol caps with the mixture and bake, face up, in a medium oven for 15 minutes. They may also be sliced and preserved by either pickling or freezing.

Habitat: *Amongst grass in pastures, open woodland and roadside verges, sometimes in fairy rings.*

LOOKALIKES

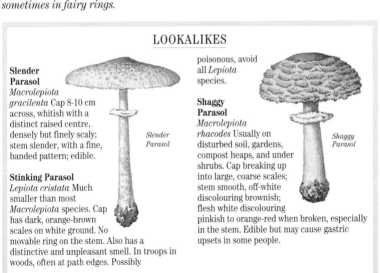

Slender Parasol
Macrolepiota gracilenta Cap 8-10 cm across, whitish with a distinct raised centre, densely but finely scaly; stem slender, with a fine, banded pattern; edible.

Slender Parasol

Stinking Parasol
Lepiota cristata Much smaller than most *Macrolepiota* species. Cap has dark, orange-brown scales on white ground. No movable ring on the stem. Also has a distinctive and unpleasant smell. In troops in woods, often at path edges. Possibly poisonous, avoid all *Lepiota* species.

Shaggy Parasol
Macrolepiota rhacodes Usually on disturbed soil, gardens, compost heaps, and under shrubs. Cap breaking up into large, coarse scales; stem smooth, off-white discolouring brownish; flesh white discolouring pinkish to orange-red when broken, especially in the stem. Edible but may cause gastric upsets in some people.

Shaggy Parasol

195

Shaggy Ink Cap

Shaggy Ink Cap
Coprinus comatus

Use
Treat these delicate mushrooms with care. Immeditaly slice in half lengthwise and fry in butter for two minutes. Serve on toast with plenty of black pepper.

Gills free, white becoming grey then black from the edge, and dissolving into a black ink; very densely crowded

Cap tall and cylindrical with a rounded top, only expanding slightly as it matures, pure white except for a pale brown apex, breaking up into tiers of curled, woolly scales, dry, blackening and dissolving upwards from the margin as the gills liquefy, or deliquesce

Tall cylindrical cap, tiers of white curly scales

Spore print

Stem cylindrical, white, hollow, with a movable ring towards the base

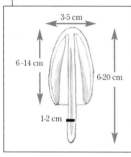

3-5 cm

6 -14 cm

6-20 cm

1-2 cm

A distinctive mushroom, unlikely to be confused with any poisonous species. It is found in fields, road verges and mown lawns from spring to late autumn, sometimes in very large numbers. These mushrooms are delicious, but need to be picked in the early morning, as they soon deteriorate. Choose very young specimens, in which the gills are still totally white, and have not yet started to blacken.

COOKING AND EATING Shaggy Ink Caps are still quite edible when very young (see above) but the black 'ink' (caused by the ripe spores) is a little off-putting, and they dissolve, or 'deliquesce', once picked, so should be eaten within one or two hours. They are extremely fragile, but also flavoursome: take advantage of this quality by making a quick soup. It is a good idea to have some other, more robust mushrooms to bulk it out a little. In a saucepan, gently soften some finely chopped onion in a little butter. Add about 250 g of chopped Shaggy Ink Caps and a little garlic, and allow these to soften. Then add 1 litre of hot chicken stock, simmer for 15 minutes, and liquidize the soup. Meanwhile, fry some other chopped mushrooms, such as Field Mushrooms or Parasols, and add. Finish off with half a cup of double cream, seasoning, and chopped parsley.

Habitat: Commonly found in grassland and parkland, sometimes in very large numbers, and frequently emerging between paving stones in towns.

LOOKALIKES

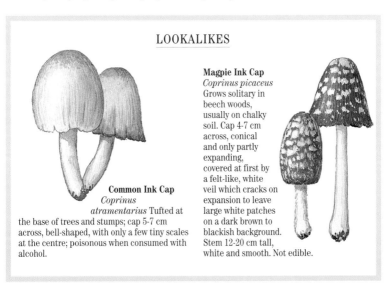

Magpie Ink Cap
Coprinus picaceus
Grows solitary in beech woods, usually on chalky soil. Cap 4-7 cm across, conical and only partly expanding, covered at first by a felt-like, white veil which cracks on expansion to leave large white patches on a dark brown to blackish background. Stem 12-20 cm tall, white and smooth. Not edible.

Common Ink Cap
Coprinus atramentarius Tufted at the base of trees and stumps; cap 5-7 cm across, bell-shaped, with only a few tiny scales at the centre; poisonous when consumed with alcohol.

Field Mushroom

Field Mushroom
Agaricus campestris

Grassland species; pink gills turning
chocolate brown, small ring on stem; flesh
discolours pink, no yellow bruising

Cap strongly convex, becoming almost
flattened, pure white or sometimes with
greyish-brown tints at the centre; dry, smooth
or indistinctly scaly in old specimens

Use
Open specimens of this delicious
species should be treated simply
– fry in plenty of butter on both
sides and serve on toast.

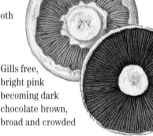

Gills free,
bright pink
becoming dark
chocolate brown,
broad and crowded

Stem short and
cylindrical or tapering
at the base; white,
smooth, bearing a
small, thin ring which
quickly disappears on
weathering

Spore print

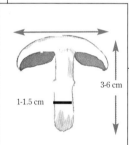

3-6 cm

1-1.5 cm

This, the best-known edible mushroom, is familiar to
most people because it is the one usually illustrated
in biology textbooks. It has a pleasant smell, and a nutti-
er flavour than the commercially cultivated mushroom. It
can be identified primarily by the attractive rose-pink gills
of just-opened specimens, the slightly reddening flesh, and the small, simple ring on
the stem. It is often associated with horse pasture, and it is well-worth investigating
likely fields for them in late summer, early in the morning when there is still some dew
on the grass, and no-one else has beaten you to it.

COOKING AND EATING Field Mushrooms can be treated in much the same way as shop-
bought, cultivated mushrooms, which are derived from a closely-related species,
Agaricus bisporus. However, the flavour is definitely superior, so avoid adding too
many other tastes and textures that may mask its qualities. If you can find some young
specimens, trim off the stems and coat them with beaten egg. Then roll them in a mixture of breadcrumbs and flour in equal quantities, seasoned liberally with salt, pepper,
and dried Thyme and Marjoram leaves. Shake off the excess, and deep fry in vegetable
oil, one or two at a time, draining the fried mushrooms on paper towels. Serve with a
salad of Chickweed and Dandelion leaves, dressed with olive oil and lemon juice.

Habitat: *scattered in open grassland.*

LOOKALIKES

Cultivated Mushroom
Agaricus bisporus The pure white form is mostly grown commercially, but in the wild this uncommon species typically has brown, fibrous scales on the cap. Otherwise differs from the field mushroom in the much larger, less ephemeral ring, and the flesh not reddening so quickly.

Yellow Stainer
Agaricus xanthoderma Easily mistaken for the Field Mushroom or the Horse Mushroom, but the surface stains bright yellow, and is especially yellow in the flesh at the stem base. Also has a large, membranous ring, and an unpleasant smell. One of the few poisonous *Agaricus* species.

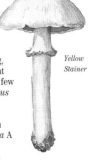

Wood Mushroom
Agaricus silvicola A white to cream mushroom with a smooth cap, a swollen stem base and a thin ring; bruises yellow and has a smell of aniseed. Found in woodland, not grassland. Edible, but do not confuse with the deadly Destroying Angel.

Cep or Penny Bun

Penny Bun
Boletus edulis

Use
Ceps and other Boletes dry extremely well if cut into thin slices. Reconstitute them by covering with boiling water and leaving for at least 30 minutes. Be sure to use the intensely-flavoured liquor too.

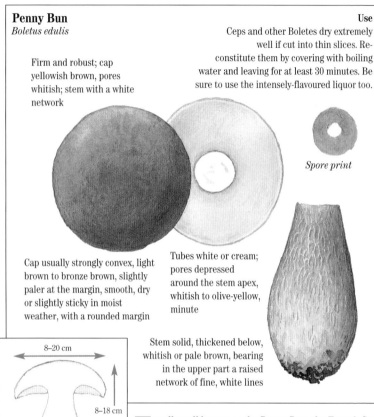

Firm and robust; cap yellowish brown, pores whitish; stem with a white network

Spore print

Cap usually strongly convex, light brown to bronze brown, slightly paler at the margin, smooth, dry or slightly sticky in moist weather, with a rounded margin

Tubes white or cream; pores depressed around the stem apex, whitish to olive-yellow, minute

Stem solid, thickened below, whitish or pale brown, bearing in the upper part a raised network of fine, white lines

8–20 cm

8–18 cm

4–7 cm

Equally well known as the Penny Bun, the French Cep, or the Italian Porcini, this is surely one of the most prized wild mushrooms of all. A warm season, with plentiful rain can produce a 'bolete year', when they grow abundantly. Its firm flesh prevents early rotting, but older specimens may contain insect larvae. Fruitbodies are frequently dried for later use in soups, or may be pickled.

COOKING AND EATING They have tender, juicy flesh with a delicate, distinctive flavour, which intensifies on drying. Ideally they should be picked when the spongy tube layer is still white, but if it has begun to yellow, it can be removed before cooking. They can be used to improve the flavour of other species, are excellent in a risotto, or served in a cream sauce with a wide-ribbon pasta, such as pappardelle. They are the perfect soup-mushroom, and are used for this purpose commercially. Fry a little onion and garlic in butter until it has begins to brown. Add a handful of Ceps, and an equal amount of a blander species such as Field Mushroom or the shop-bought variety. Continue to cook until they soften, and then add as much beef stock as appropriate, with chopped marjoram. Simmer for about 15 minutes, then blend. Add single cream and serve with bread.

Habitat: *On the ground in pine, oak and chestnut woods.*

LOOKALIKES

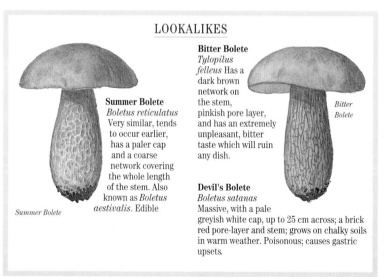

Summer Bolete
Boletus reticulatus
Very similar, tends
to occur earlier,
has a paler cap
and a coarse
network covering
the whole length
of the stem. Also
known as *Boletus
aestivalis*. Edible

Summer Bolete

Bitter Bolete
*Tylopilus
felleus* Has a
dark brown
network on
the stem,
pinkish pore layer,
and has an extremely
unpleasant, bitter
taste which will ruin
any dish.

*Bitter
Bolete*

Devil's Bolete
Boletus satanas
Massive, with a pale
greyish white cap, up to 25 cm across; a brick
red pore-layer and stem; grows on chalky soils
in warm weather. Poisonous; causes gastric
upsets.

Bay Bolete

Bay Bolete
Boletus badius

Dark chestnut brown cap; yellowish pores, bluing flesh; slender stem

Use
Drying Bay Boletes intensifies their flavour. If you use dried ones for the risotto below, use the liquid they've been reconstituted in for the stock.

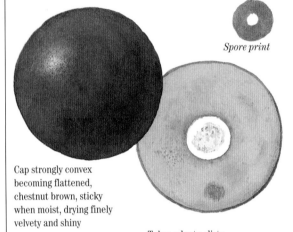

Spore print

Cap strongly convex becoming flattened, chestnut brown, sticky when moist, drying finely velvety and shiny

Tubes adnate, dirty yellow, quickly bruising to bluish green when touched

Stem cylindrical or tapering below, paler than cap, fibrous, lacking any net or granules

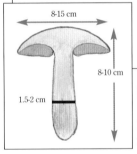

8-15 cm

8-10 cm

1.5-2 cm

The Bay Bolete is characterised by its rather slender stem and yellowish pore surface, which immediately turns blue with a thumbprint. The yellowish-white flesh also turns pale blue on exposure to air, but only slightly, and over a longer period. It has a distinctive flavour, and is regarded by some as equal to the Cep, but has a milder taste. It makes an excellent risotto, especially if mixed with other 'brown' mushrooms.

COOKING AND EATING Gently fry the sliced mushrooms in butter for a minute or two until they start to go soft. Remove from the pan, and, in the same pan, fry some finely-chopped onion and garlic. Prepare about 600 ml of vegetable or chicken stock, and leave to simmer in a saucepan. When the onions are soft, add a cup of risotto rice (such as Arborio or Carnaroli) and stir, continuing to fry until the rice looks translucent – but do not let it brown. Add a small glass of white wine, and boil until it has been absorbed. Add ladlefulls of the simmering stock one at a time, stirring all the while, until the rice is cooked – it should be moist and creamy with a little 'bite' in the centre of the grain. Return the mushrooms to the rice with some chopped parsley, and check for seasoning. Finally, stir some grated parmesan on to the risotto and serve.

J F M A M J J A **S** **O** N D

Habitat: *On ground in both leafy and coniferous woodland.*

LOOKALIKES

Lurid Bolete

Lurid Bolete
Boletus luridus
Under beech and oak, on chalky soil. Cap convex, yellowish brown; stem swollen, red, with a coarse network, flesh turns violet to blue-green when broken open. Poisonous when eaten raw or undercooked.

Yellow-cracked Bolete
Xerocomus subtomentosus
One of the most common boletes, in mixed, open woodland. Cap 4-8 cm across, yellowish brown, dry and velvety; pores golden yellow, stem slender, finely ridged. Edible but not recommended.

Yellow-cracked Bolete

Red-cracked Bolete
Xerocomus chrysenteron Similar to the yellow-cracked bolete, but cap with carmine red cracks. Edible as above.

Slippery Jack

Slippery Jack
Suillus luteus

Cap dark brown, slimy, pores
lemon yellow; stem with a
large ring

Caution

As with all the species of *Suillus*, the cap is
covered by a slimy surface layer called the
pellicle. This layer must be peeled away
before cooking the mushroom, as it can
cause unpleasant gastric upsets.

Spore print

Cap convex, very slimy, dull
chestnut brown or chocolate
brown with purplish tinge

Tubes adnate, pale yellow;
pores small, lemon yellow
or straw coloured

Stem brownish below, whitish or pale
yellowish above, with brownish,
glandular dots below the ring; ring
large, spreading, membranous, cream
or yellowish, darkening as the spores
are released from the pore surface

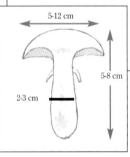

5-12 cm

5-8 cm

2-3 cm

The Slippery Jack is a pinewood species, particularly
common among Scots pine on sandy ground where it
can appear in large numbers – although it is often hidden
by fallen pines-needles. The mushroom is characterized by
the very slimy, chestnut cap and well-developed ring. It is
best collected in late season when there is little risk of insect attack. The flavour is good,
comparable with the Penny Bun, page 200, but the flesh softens considerably in cooking,
so Slippery Jacks are best mixed with other species in a mushroom soup.

COOKING AND EATING In a saucepan, sauté some finely chopped onion and garlic in
butter for a minute or two, then add about 200 g of very finely chopped wild mushrooms
of any species including Slippery Jack. Sauté the mushrooms for a further 3 minutes,
then add about 4 tbsp of milk and remove the pan from the heat. In a separate pan,
beat about 40 g of plain flour into 40 g of melted butter and cook gently to form a roux,
which should be just lightly browned. Remove from the heat and gradually stir in a litre
of chicken or vegetable stock, a little at a time, using a whisk to knock out any lumps.
Finally, add the mushrooms to the stock and simmer for 15 minutes, adding fresh parsley and seasoning with salt and pepper. Serve with sour cream on top, and rustic bread.

Habitat: *Under conifers, especially pines.*

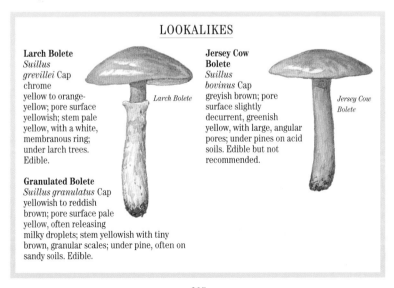

LOOKALIKES

Larch Bolete
Suillus grevillei Cap chrome yellow to orange-yellow; pore surface yellowish; stem pale yellow, with a white, membranous ring; under larch trees. Edible.

Larch Bolete

Granulated Bolete
Suillus granulatus Cap yellowish to reddish brown; pore surface pale yellow, often releasing milky droplets; stem yellowish with tiny brown, granular scales; under pine, often on sandy soils. Edible.

Jersey Cow Bolete
Suillus bovinus Cap greyish brown; pore surface slightly decurrent, greenish yellow, with large, angular pores; under pines on acid soils. Edible but not recommended.

Jersey Cow Bolete

Brown Birch Bolete

Brown Birch Bolete
Leccinum scabrum

Tip
Brown Birch Bolete has a good flavour, but is apt to become rather soft when cooked, especially the spongy pore layer which is best removed beforehand.

Tall stem with black granules; cap grey-brown, flesh stays white

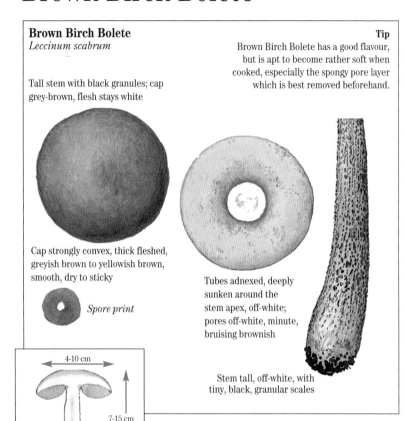

Cap strongly convex, thick fleshed, greyish brown to yellowish brown, smooth, dry to sticky

Spore print

Tubes adnexed, deeply sunken around the stem apex, off-white; pores off-white, minute, bruising brownish

Stem tall, off-white, with tiny, black, granular scales

4-10 cm

7-15 cm

2-3 cm

This is a very common species, belonging to a group of bolete-type fungi with spongy tubes instead of gills and rough, scaly stems. It is almost always found growing beneath Birch trees, sometimes in large numbers. The white flesh does not discolour when cut open, but it is often victim to insect attack, and may be riddled with maggot holes, especially in the stem. For this reason it is best to seek out young specimens, or collect them later in the year when there are fewer insects around.

COOKING AND EATING It is good mixed with other species to make a mushroom stuffing, such as in this baked pasta dish. Sauté a finely chopped onion in butter, and add a medley of chopped wild mushrooms including Brown Birch Bolete, such as Ceps, Bay Boletes, Oyster Mushrooms or Horn of Plenty. Continue to cook, until any resulting fluid has evaporated, and season. When cool, mix with a beaten egg and some breadcrumbs to bind together. Take some fresh, or pre-cooked cannelloni tubes, and stuff with the mixture. Place the cannelloni in a dish so they fit snugly, and cover with a white cheese or béchamel sauce and season with white pepper and grated nutmeg. Bake in a moderate oven for 30 minutes. Serve with wilted spinach leaves tossed in garlic butter.

Habitat: *On the ground, under birches.*

LOOKALIKES

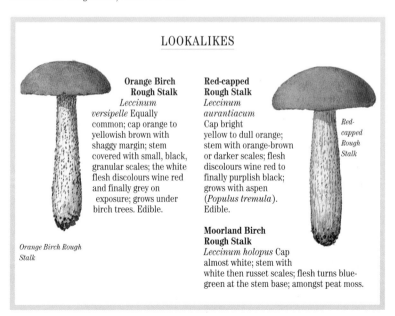

Orange Birch Rough Stalk
Leccinum versipelle Equally common; cap orange to yellowish brown with shaggy margin; stem covered with small, black, granular scales; the white flesh discolours wine red and finally grey on exposure; grows under birch trees. Edible.

Orange Birch Rough Stalk

Red-capped Rough Stalk
Leccinum aurantiacum Cap bright yellow to dull orange; stem with orange-brown or darker scales; flesh discolours wine red to finally purplish black; grows with aspen (*Populus tremula*). Edible.

Moorland Birch Rough Stalk
Leccinum holopus Cap almost white; stem with white then russet scales; flesh turns blue-green at the stem base; amongst peat moss.

Red-capped Rough Stalk

Orange Birch Bolete

Orange Birch Bolete
Leccinum versipelle

Reddish orange cap; stem with
black, granular scales; flesh
blackening on exposure

Use
Combine the mushroom paste described below
with olive oil, a little balsamic vinegar and some
fresh herbs to make a mushroom dip. Best made
with 'soft' species such as Orange Birch Bolete,
Slippery Jack and Shaggy Ink Cap.

Cap strongly convex, reddish
orange to saffron, smooth,
dry to slightly sticky when
moist, with shaggy edge

Tubes adnexed, deeply sunken
around the stem apex, yellowish
to greyish; pores off-white,
minute, bruising brownish

Spore print

Stem tall, off-white,
covered over entire
length with tiny,
black, granular
scales

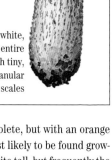

8-15 cm

7-15 cm

2-4 cm

Very like the Brown Birch Bolete, but with an orange
cap, this species is also most likely to be found growing among Birches. It is often quite tall, but frequently the
stem is riddled with insect larvae. The flavour of the cap
is good, some say almost as good as the Penny Bun, page
200, though the flesh discolours when broken, and goes quite black when cooked. This,
and the fact that it turns rather soft, makes it an ideal species to mix with other fungi
for mushroom paste, which can be used for almost anything including stuffing ravioli.

COOKING AND EATING Make the paste by frying a medley of finely chopped wild mushroom species in butter with a little garlic, until soft and any water has evaporated.
Season with salt and pepper. Make the pasta by combining 150 g of pasta flour (grade
'00'), 1 whole egg and 1 egg yolk. Use the dough hook on a food processor if you have
one, or knead the dough for at least 15 minutes, then leave to rest, covered, for at least
1 hour. Then roll the dough out, fold, and roll again – do this at least six times. Cut
the pasta into 8 cm strips, add blobs of mushroom paste 8 cm apart, and place another strip on top, sealing tightly with beaten egg and cutting the strips between the blobs
into ravioli. Cook in boiling water for 3 minutes.

Habitat: *On the ground, under birches.*

LOOKALIKES

**Poplar
Rough Stalk**
*Leccinum
duriusculum* Cap 8-15
cm across, greyish brown
to coffee brown, often
finely cracked; tubes
greyish bruising pink to
brown; stem white,
covered with fine, dark
brown, woolly scales;
flesh bruising pink to
pale violaceous. Under
poplar. An excellent edible species with a
firm to hard flesh.

*Poplar
Rough
Stalk*

Oak Rough Stalk
Leccinum quercinum Cap up to 20 cm
across, brick red to rusty orange, rather
scaly; tubes
cream to
ochraceous buff;
stem white,
covered with tiny
reddish brown to
blackish scales; flesh
bruising violaceous to
blackish. Under oak or
beech. Edible.

*Oak
Rough
Stalk*

**Yellow-cracking
Rough Stalk**
Leccinum crocipodium Cap yellowish brown
to cinnamon, velvety, conspicuously cracking;
tubes bright yellow; stem yellow, with tiny,
yellowish brown scales in lines; pale flesh
bruising blackish violaceous. Edible but
blackens when cooked.

Saffron Milk Cap

Saffron Milk Cap
Lactarius deliciosus

Large, reddish orange mushroom, bruising
green; abundant orange latex; stem pitted

Use
Fry sliced Saffron Milk Caps in oil with
onion and garlic. Season, add a dash of
cream and warm through. Mix with
Dandelion leaves.

Cap convex, soon depressed with an
incurved margin, reddish orange with
several concentric darker zones, slimy
when moist, staining green

Gills adnate to
short decurrent,
pale orange-yellow,
staining green,
crowded

Spore print

Stem short,
orange, often
pitted, staining
greenish

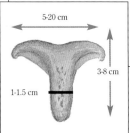

5-20 cm

3-8 cm

1-1.5 cm

There are many wild mushrooms belonging to the genus Lactarius, all characterised by exuding a milky juice from the flesh, easily seen by running a fingernail over the gills. The 'milk', or latex, may be white, yellow or orange, and often has a fiery, peppery taste – but all Lactarius are best avoided as they are potentially poisonous – except for the Saffron Milk Cap. It is very easily identified by the orange latex which turns green on drying. It is highly regarded in some parts of Europe, and is even sold in markets. In Eastern Europe it is often pickled. Saffron Milk Caps have a fairly mild flavour, but a firm texture and the orange colour remains intact even after cooking, so they are best used in dishes where the colour can be appreciated. They can certainly be mixed quite happily with other species in a mushroom medley.

COOKING AND EATING To pickle, bring 1 cup of white wine vinegar and half a cup of water to simmer in a saucepan. Add salt, peppercorns, chopped fresh or dried chilli flakes and some coriander seeds. Add the mushrooms – young ones are best, and cook for 10 minutes. Spoon into sealable, sterilized jars, making sure that the liquid reaches the top. Or, fill the jar with olive oil instead of the pickling vinegar.

Habitat: *Often in large numbers under conifers, especially pines.*

LOOKALIKES

Bloody Milk Cap
Lactarius sanguifluus Cap 9-12 cm across, reddish, with pinkish vinaceous zones, powdery, only slightly discolouring green; gills vinaceous pink; stem reddish-purple, with vinaceous pits; the red-vinaceous flesh releases a similarly coloured latex. Under pine, more common in France.

Bloody Milk Cap

Woolly Milk Cap
Lactarius torminosus A common species found under birch in wet places. Cap shaggy and woolly, with concentric pinkish zones; exuding a white, very acrid latex, and a smell of pelargonium. Inedible.

Woolly Milk Cap

Liquorice Milk Cap
Lactarius helvus Occasional under conifers; cap greyish yellow-brown, with paler yellow gills and a hollow stem The flesh gives out a clear, watery latex and a liquorice smell, especially when dried. Tastes mild, but is poisonous.

Charcoal Burner

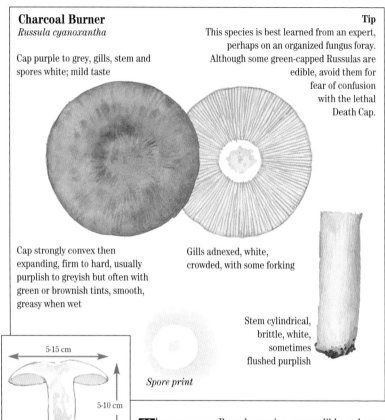

Charcoal Burner
Russula cyanoxantha

Cap purple to grey, gills, stem and spores white; mild taste

Tip
This species is best learned from an expert, perhaps on an organized fungus foray. Although some green-capped Russulas are edible, avoid them for fear of confusion with the lethal Death Cap.

Cap strongly convex then expanding, firm to hard, usually purplish to greyish but often with green or brownish tints, smooth, greasy when wet

Gills adnexed, white, crowded, with some forking

Stem cylindrical, brittle, white, sometimes flushed purplish

Spore print

5-15 cm

5-10 cm

1-3 cm

There are many Russula species, some edible and some not, either because they are too peppery or, as with the Bright Scarlet or pink ones (*Russula emetica*), because they cause gastric upset. The Charcoal Burner is the best of the edible Russulas, and although its appearance is variable, it is reasonably easy to identify once you have some experience with this difficult group. It is very common, usually purplish- or bluish-grey, often with a yellowish centre; the white gills break easily if touched. It often appears early in the season, from July onwards. In mainland Europe, the species is often called the Parrot Russula, because of its colour variation. It is also known by the unimaginative name of Blue-Yellow Brittle Gill, which describes it well enough. How it comes to be called the Charcoal Burner is unclear: maybe it was a regular food of forest charcoal-makers. A drawback to the Russulas is their attraction to slugs: those appearing early in the season are often decimated by the time you pick them.

COOKING AND EATING The Charcoal Burner is a firm mushroom that retains its texture after cooking, and has a pleasantly nutty flavour, though mild. They are excellent mixed with other, more fully-flavoured fungi to help bulk out a dish, such as a risotto.

Habitat: *Troops in leafy woods and parkland.*

LOOKALIKES

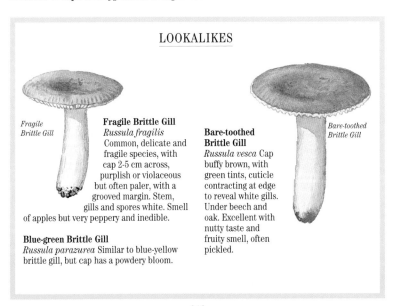

Fragile Brittle Gill

Fragile Brittle Gill
Russula fragilis
Common, delicate and fragile species, with cap 2-5 cm across, purplish or violaceous but often paler, with a grooved margin. Stem, gills and spores white. Smell of apples but very peppery and inedible.

Bare-toothed Brittle Gill
Russula vesca Cap buffy brown, with green tints, cuticle contracting at edge to reveal white gills. Under beech and oak. Excellent with nutty taste and fruity smell, often pickled.

Bare-toothed Brittle Gill

Blue-green Brittle Gill
Russula parazurea Similar to blue-yellow brittle gill, but cap has a powdery bloom.

213

Giant Puffball

Giant Puffball
Calvatia gigantea

Tip
Giant Puffballs must be in peak condition for eating. Before collecting, cut a small slice deep into the flesh, which should be white and firm like marshmallow. If it is at all yellow or brown, it is too late.

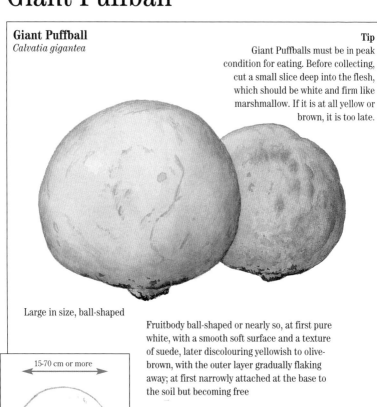

Large in size, ball-shaped

15-70 cm or more

Fruitbody ball-shaped or nearly so, at first pure white, with a smooth soft surface and a texture of suede, later discolouring yellowish to olive-brown, with the outer layer gradually flaking away; at first narrowly attached at the base to the soil but becoming free

The Giant Puffball is probably the easiest of all the fungi to recognize. The fruitbodies can often be spotted for hundreds of metres away, like white abandoned footballs discarded after a puncture. They can weigh as much as 20 kg, and 4 kg is frequently recorded. They are not always common, so finding one should be treated as an exciting privilege, but in some years they can be found in large numbers, when they may form fairy rings in open woodland, in grassland or on disturbed soil, such as roadsides or embankments near hedges. They often seem to be associated with Stinging Nettles. Finding an old specimen – the large spherical tissue of brown sponge that releases millions of spores when kicked – signals a lost opportunity.

COOKING AND EATING They are delicious enough to treat very simply. The slightly leathery, though perfectly edible, skin can be peeled off first if desired. Cut the firm white flesh into slices 1 cm thick, sprinkle with salt and pepper and a pinch of Marjoram leaves and fry in butter or, better still, bacon fat. The slices may be coated in beaten egg and breadcrumbs for a crisper finish. Many other smaller puffballs are edible in their young condition.

Habitat: *Singly or in groups, sometimes forming large fairy rings, in fields and on road verges.*

LOOKALIKES

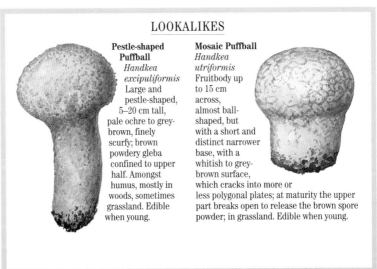

Pestle-shaped Puffball
Handkea excipuliformis
Large and pestle-shaped, 5–20 cm tall, pale ochre to grey-brown, finely scurfy; brown powdery gleba confined to upper half. Amongst humus, mostly in woods, sometimes grassland. Edible when young.

Mosaic Puffball
Handkea utriformis
Fruitbody up to 15 cm across, almost ball-shaped, but with a short and distinct narrower base, with a whitish to grey-brown surface, which cracks into more or less polygonal plates; at maturity the upper part breaks open to release the brown spore powder; in grassland. Edible when young.

Jew's Ear

Jew's Ear
Auricularia auricula-judae

Use
In dry weather, pick the dried-up fruit bodies from elder trees and soak them in warm water for a couple of hours, when they will increase hugely in volume, either for culinary use or to amuse your friends.

Approximate size and shape of a human ear; jelly-like

Fertile surface (inner) greyish brown, usually wrinkled or veined, otherwise smooth and shiny

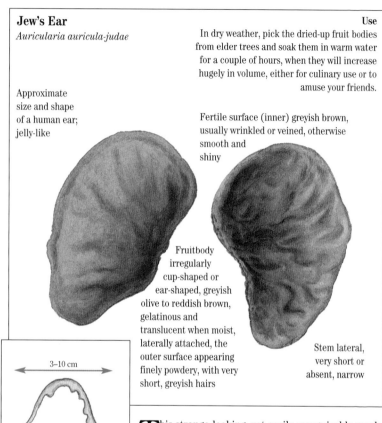

Fruitbody irregularly cup-shaped or ear-shaped, greyish olive to reddish brown, gelatinous and translucent when moist, laterally attached, the outer surface appearing finely powdery, with very short, greyish hairs

Stem lateral, very short or absent, narrow

3–10 cm

This strange-looking, yet easily recognizable mushroom grows on the branches of several species of tree, but particularly on Elder and Sycamore. The fruitbody is gelatinous or rubbery to the touch, and usually grows in clusters.

COOKING AND EATING The Jew's Ear is widely used in stir-fry dishes and soups in Chinese cuisine, probably more for its chewy texture than its flavour – it is rather lacking in taste, and requires gentle cooking to tenderize the rubbery flesh. Clean the ears well to get rid of any insects or bits of bark that are stuck to them, then cut them into strips and stir-fry with crunchier vegetables and noodles and flavour with soy or oyster sauce. They work particularly well in a variation on the classic Thai soup, Tom Yam Goong. Bring to the boil 1 litre of fish stock. Add some bruised stalks of Lemon Grass, some Kaffir Lime Leaves, and pieces of Galangal root, then simmer for 5 minutes. Strain the stock, add 6–8 halved Jew's Ears and a few baby sweetcorn and simmer for a further 5 minutes. Then add some cooked peeled prawns, 2 tablespoons fish sauce, the juice of 1 lime, 1 chopped red chilli, 2 chopped spring onions and some torn coriander leaves. Serve immediately – it should be spicy, salty and sour.

Habitat: *Clustered on dead branches, especially of elder and elm, preferring damp. warm localities.*

LOOKALIKES

Tripe fungus

Tripe Fungus
Auricularia mesenterica A common species distinguished by the gelatinous, bracket-like fruitbodies which have a densely hairy upper surface, with alternating zones of grey and brown. The fertile (lower) surface is reddish-purple, smooth or veined; on stumps and logs of leafy trees, especially elm. Not edible.

Silver Leaf Fungus
Chondrostereum purpureum Has similar, shaggy brackets and purplish fertile surface, but is not gelatinous. Weakly parasitic, a disease of plum trees, causing the leaves to turn silver. Inedible.

Winter

The leanest time of year, but one for enjoying wild food already gathered and preserved. Nuts, fruits and mushrooms taste great in the depths of winter.

There are plenty of shellfish on the seashore – time your visit to coincide with the lowest tides and be sure to read the advice in the Introduction, page 14.

Hardy leaves such as Dandelion, White Dead-Nettle and Watercress are still available, and soon the fresh shoots of Alexanders will be sprouting.

◁ *White Dead-nettle*

Watercress

Velvet Shank

Mussels

Dandelion

Fat Hen

Fat Hen
Chenopodium album

Use
It is the seeds of Fat Hen that provide the nourishment cherished by early man, as they contain high levels of carbohydrate and protein.

The flowers are a dense collection of tiny greenish-grey blobs, too small to be worthy of close examination.

Leaves are more or less diamond-shaped, though much narrower at the top of the plant, with a coarsely toothed margin.

Wasteland

Fat Hen, or the remains of it, has been found at archaeological sites of prehistoric settlements all over Europe, indicating that it has long been established as a useful plant. It is often the first plant to grow on recently cultivated ground, especially if the ground has been manured or well fertilized. It crops up on wasteland or neglected arable fields, or close to building sites, but may easily be passed by as an unprepossessing weed. It may be confused with Common Orache, which has thicker grey leaves with a mealy surface, but this is also edible. It is one of the most worthwhile of leafy edible wild plants.

COOKING AND EATING The leaves and young flowering shoots make an excellent substitute for Kale or Broccoli, provided they are cooked, but the young shoots that sprout up at almost any time of the year may be eaten raw, or briefly blanched or steamed and tossed in butter, then mixed with chunks of well-flavoured cooked sausage, such as wild boar. Larger leaves may be cooked, mixed together with some mashed potato and an egg and.fried to make bubble and squeak. Season with pepper, salt and nutmeg. The nutritious seeds may be sprouted and eaten fresh, or ground into a flour and baked on a hot plate as an unleavened, flat bread.

Fat Hen *is an unprepossessing knee-high plant, with few distinguishing features save the clumps of tiny, greyish flowers. It often forms quite extensive colonies, with other arable weeds, but always where the soil has been enriched and disturbed.*

Fat Hen

RANGE: Throughout Europe.

HABITAT: Wasteland, neglected arable fields.

FLOWERING TIME: June to October.

Watercress

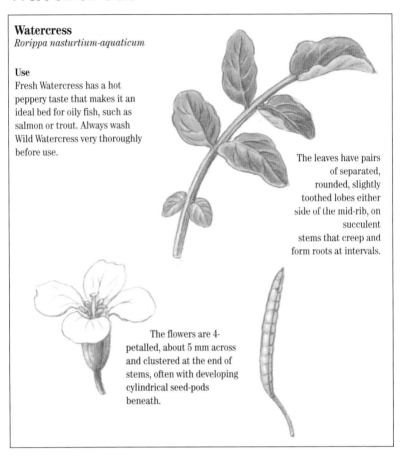

Watercress
Rorippa nasturtium-aquaticum

Use
Fresh Watercress has a hot peppery taste that makes it an ideal bed for oily fish, such as salmon or trout. Always wash Wild Watercress very thoroughly before use.

The leaves have pairs of separated, rounded, slightly toothed lobes either side of the mid-rib, on succulent stems that creep and form roots at intervals.

The flowers are 4-petalled, about 5 mm across and clustered at the end of stems, often with developing cylindrical seed-pods beneath.

Ponds

Watercress is easily identified by its four cress-type petals when in flower. It is found at the margins of fast-flowing streams or in ditches and ponds. The green parts, however, are very similar to some other species, particularly of the carrot family. Watercress and its various hybrids are the same as watercress sold commercially and used in salads, but it should not be collected in the wild for culinary use if there are livestock grazing nearby or upstream, unless it is thoroughly cooked: it may contain the larvae of liver flukes, which can infect humans as well as cattle and sheep.

COOKING AND EATING Watercress begins to flower in early summer, but as the leaves are protected by their watery habitat from frost, they are available for most of the year. Watercress soup is the classic dish and simple to make. Sautée some chopped potatoes very gently in a covered pan with a little butter and a dash of vegetable oil for 10 minutes, stirring frequently (the oil prevents the butter from burning). Add some chicken or vegetable stock, and simmer until the potatoes are almost cooked. Then add a generous bunch of well-washed watercress and simmer for a further 5 minutes. Blend he soup until smooth, stir in some cream and season with salt and pepper. Serve hot or chilled.

Watercress *is a succulent plant that always has its feet in water, growing to somewhere between ankle- and knee-height. The 4-petalled flowers distinguish it from other plants with similar leaves.*

Watercress

RANGE: Throughout Europe, except for much of Scandinavia.

HABITAT: Fast-flowing streams, ponds, ditches.

FLOWERING TIME: May to October.

Alexanders

Alexanders
Smyrnium olusatrum

Leaves divided into three groups of three flat, rounded or oval leaflets, with a coarsely toothed margin. They are flimsy in texture when young, and bright yellow green, becoming tougher and darker as they mature. They are arranged alternately on the stem towards the bottom of the plant, but in opposite pairs higher up.

The tiny, five-petalled greenish-yellow flowers are borne in tight, domed umbels 4-8 cm across. They should be picked just as the buds are opening.

Use
Cut the young stems, strip off the leaves, and peel away the stringy, outer layer with a knife or potato peeler. Cut into long chunks and steam or simmer for a few minutes, serving immediately with butter and black pepper – delicious.

Coast

Many seaside and coastal plants come into their own in late summer, when the air has warmed up, but Alexanders announces the spring thoroughly with a flourish. The bright, yellowish-green clumps are unmistakeable, and this is the time to take advantage of their abundance, when the shoots are still fresh and tender. Any later in the year, and all the parts become bitter.

COOKING AND EATING The whole plant is edible, though the young stems are the best part and worth eating on their own. The leaves may also be used, a few tossed into a salad to give a mild aniseed flavour. For a more substantial dish, collect a few of the flowerheads. Choose the most compact, with the buds just bursting, and avoid any that are turning to seed. Shake them clean of the numerous small insects that are attracted to this early supply of nectar, and briefly blanch them in boiling water. Then toss them with some fried, smoked bacon or cubes of *pancetta*, and if available, a few chopped Ramsons leaves which should just start to wilt in the steam. Alternatively, coat in a light batter made with 150 g of plain flour sieved with 15 g baking powder, and enough water to make a fairly thin liquid, and deep fry them to make Alexanders fritters.

Alexanders *is a robust, leafy plant, forming clumps that reach waist- to chest height. There may be great drifts of it on embankments or estuaries and cliffs close to the sea, and sometimes along roads inland. Avoid picking any that may be regularly exposed to exhaust fumes.*

Alexanders

RANGE: Coastal regions of France, Holland, southern Britain and Ireland.

HABITAT: Embankments, estuaries and seaside cliffs.

FLOWERING TIME: April to June.

White Dead-Nettle

White Dead-Nettle
Lamium album

Use
Chopped Dead-Nettle leaves go well when mixed with starchy foods such as rice and couscous. Try mixing small strips with polenta dough, deep or shallow fried.

The leaves are shaped like those of Stinging Nettle: heart shaped, with coarse teeth and in opposite pairs on a square stem.

The two-lipped flowers are 20-25 mm long, with the upper lip forming a distinct hood, occuring in whorls above each pair of the upper leaves.

Hedgerows

White Dead-Nettle is a common plant of road verges, hedgerows and woodland margins, that is easy to recognize as soon as it bursts into flower. But until that happens, the harmless leaves alone look remarkably like those of the Stinging Nettle, with which it often grows, although the two are unrelated. No doubt this resemblance helps to protect the plant from being grazed or even pulled up as a weed. The whorls of large white, two-lipped flowers are visited by bumble bees, which have the body weight to push apart the lips of the flower and reach the nectar at their base.

COOKING AND EATING The leaves may be used in exactly the same way as those of Stinging Nettle. The plants will repeatedly throw up new shoots if cut down, and may commonly be seen flowering in November. It is another plant to add to the salad arsenal of Chickweed, Ground Elder and Dandelion, provided that young shoots are used. Older leaves may be wilted with spinach-type plants such as Fat Hen, Alexanders and Sea Beet. It may also be made into a nourishing soup: soften carrot, onion and celery in butter, add generous handfuls of Deadnettle leaves and vegetable stock. Thicken with cooked rice, liquidise and season with pepper and nutmeg.

White Dead-Nettle *generally has a rather neat, tidy and lush appearance, usually about 30 cm high and in small clumps. The large flowers separate it from any other white-flowered member of the mint family.*

White Dead-Nettle

RANGE: Throughout Europe, except the far North.

HABITAT Road verges, hedgerows and woodland margins.

FLOWERING TIME April to November.

Cornsalad

Cornsalad
Valerianella locusta

Use

Cornsalad may be cooked briefly for use in soups, combining well with Chickweed, Hairy Bittercress and Wood Sorrel. Liquidize the result in a blender, season with salt and pepper, and stir in some single cream.

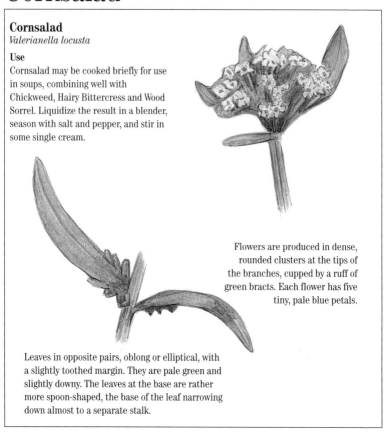

Flowers are produced in dense, rounded clusters at the tips of the branches, cupped by a ruff of green bracts. Each flower has five tiny, pale blue petals.

Leaves in opposite pairs, oblong or elliptical, with a slightly toothed margin. They are pale green and slightly downy. The leaves at the base are rather more spoon-shaped, the base of the leaf narrowing down almost to a separate stalk.

Farmland

Cornsalad is also known in Britain as Lamb's Lettuce, which gives a clue to the best time to gather it – during the lambing season. It is an early flowering annual, and, if left until after the flowers have faded, will start to wither and die, the leaves having performed their function. It was formerly widely grown as a salad vegetable, and is now experiencing a revival in the prepared bags of salad leaves available in supermarkets. It is, however, fairly common in the wild, though not always easy to spot, as the flowers are rather understated and the whole plant may have disappeared by the time summer arrives. It usually grows close to human habitation, on disturbed soils, with a particular liking for old walls. The leaves are soft and finely downy, wilting quickly but with a pleasant, refreshing flavour.

COOKING AND EATING Their texture combines well with fruit. Add to a bowl of Cornsalad leaves some peeled and sliced pears and a few walnut pieces. Make a dressing of 4 parts sunflower or grapeseed oil, 1 part olive oil and 1 part balsamic vinegar, and season with salt, pepper and mustard. Top the salad with shavings of parmesan cheese. The short harvesting season of Cornsalad can be extended almost throughout the year by sowing the seed at regular intervals in the garden.

Cornsalad *grows to ankle height, or a little higher, in disturbed or bare soils on field margins and old walls. The tiny flowers may be produced in such profusion as to give a colony of plants the impression, at a distance, of a bluish mist. It is best to strip the leaves from the stems, which can be a little bristly.*

Cornsalad

RANGE: Throughout Western and Southern Europe as far north as southern Britain.

HABITAT: Farmland.

FLOWERING TIME: April to June.

Dandelion

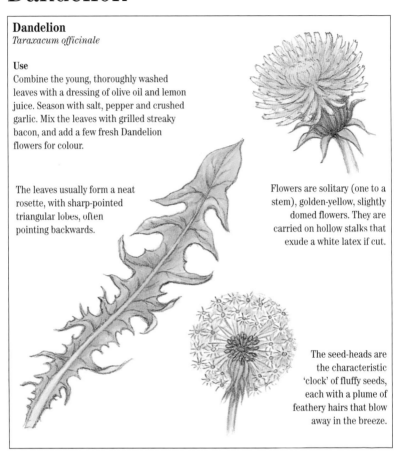

Dandelion
Taraxacum officinale

Use
Combine the young, thoroughly washed leaves with a dressing of olive oil and lemon juice. Season with salt, pepper and crushed garlic. Mix the leaves with grilled streaky bacon, and add a few fresh Dandelion flowers for colour.

The leaves usually form a neat rosette, with sharp-pointed triangular lobes, often pointing backwards.

Flowers are solitary (one to a stem), golden-yellow, slightly domed flowers. They are carried on hollow stalks that exude a white latex if cut.

The seed-heads are the characteristic 'clock' of fluffy seeds, each with a plume of feathery hairs that blow away in the breeze.

All habitats

The Dandelion is surely the most familiar of the yellow daisies, and though it may be in flower at almost any time of year, there is always a spring 'flush' when whole fields and pastures, even garden lawns, may be covered with them. Dandelions are ubiquitous, and owe their success in part to their long flowering period, but also to the fact that they set viable seed without the need for cross-fertilization with another plant. Over thousands of years this has led to particular strains, or variations, remaining stable without change, and botanists recognise many hundreds of 'subspecies'. Dandelion is one of the most useful of edible wild plants, and would perhaps be grown commercially were it not for its reputation as a diuretic, so it is best eaten in moderation.

COOKING AND EATING The younger leaves make an excellent addition to any salad, and can be made more tender if you place a cardboard tube over the young plant, so that they are blanched and grow longer. The very young buds can be preserved in white wine vinegar as a substitute for capers, as can the buds of the Common Daisy. A passable coffee is made by drying the washed roots for a few days until they are brittle. Chop these up, roast in a low oven for half an hour, and then grind them for a coffee with a difference.

Dandelion *rarely grows above ankle-height, often shorter, and creates a great show of golden, domed flower-heads in spring. The leaves, with their large, backward-pointing teeth, are familiar enough and easily identified even when the plant is not in flower, so a few leaves can be gathered at almost any time of year.*

Dandelion

RANGE: Throughout Europe.

HABITAT: Ubiquitous.

FLOWERING TIME: March to October or longer,
but particularly in spring.

Truffles

White Truffle
Tuber magnatum

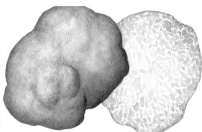

Use
Make your own truffle oil by slicing a Périgord Truffle. Put it into a bottle of the finest olive oil, and leave for several weeks. Perfect for dressing salads and simple pasta dishes.

Resembes a knobbly potato, grows underground; strong aromatic smell

Fruitbody rather irregular in form resembling a potato, often knobbly, yellowish-brown, smooth, or somewhat cracking

Périgord Truffle
Tuber melanosporum

Hard, black ball with pyramidal warts; flesh greyish changing to reddish and finally black; strong pungent odour; underground

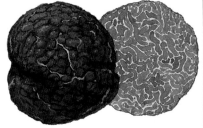

Fruitbody ball-shaped, sometimes flattened or knobbly, with a reddish to dull black surface bearing numerous small, pyramidal warts

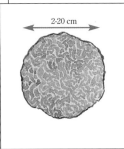

2-20 cm

On these two pages are featured all the different truffles found in Europe. Truffles are the most highly prized of edible fungi and, weight for weight, can be the world's most expensive food. This is a reflection of their unique flavour, their rarity, and the difficulty finding them. Truffles grow underground in association with the roots of trees such as oak and hazel growing on chalky soil. Specially trained dogs are used to sniff out the fungi. Pigs were used in the past, but they tend to eat what they find. It is sometimes possible to spot the location of truffles – small flies often hover just above the ground surface.

COOKING AND EATING The Summer Truffle (*Tuber aestivum*) grows in most of Europe including Britain, but has the mildest flavour and is not very highly regarded (see opposite). The almost identical-looking Périgord Truffle (*Tuber melanosporum*) prefers the warmer climes of southern Europe, and is greatly esteemed in France. The White Truffle (*Tuber magnatum*), confined to the Piemonte/Umbria region of Italy, is the most sought-after of all, with a strong, spicy odour and flavour. The Périgord and White Truffle are both harvested in winter. Thinly sliced, they are typically incorporated into patés, or placed under the skins of roasted poultry. The best way to eat them of all is to add wafer-thin slices to cooked pasta with just an olive oil and garlic dressing.

Habitat: *Grows under oak trees, occasionally chestnut or hazel, about 3-20 cm deep in alkaline soil.*

LOOKALIKES

Summer Truffle

Hart's Truffle

Summer Truffle
Tuber aestivum Grows in chalky soil, often associated with beech trees; fairly common in Britain, formerly collected by professional truffle hunters. Fruitbody 3-9 cm across, blackish brown, with prominent wart-like scales; flesh at first whitish becoming olive brown, and marbled with white veins. Smell and flavour milder than Périgord Truffle.

Hart's Truffle
Elaphomyces granulatus An underground truffle, widespread in both leafy and conifer woods, sometimes found on the surface amongst leaf litter. About 4 cm across, yellowish brown with granular surface, flesh pinkish buff developing a black, powdery spore mass. Inedible.

Oyster Mushroom

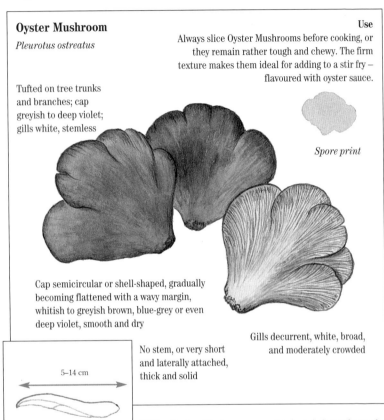

Oyster Mushroom

Pleurotus ostreatus

Use

Always slice Oyster Mushrooms before cooking, or they remain rather tough and chewy. The firm texture makes them ideal for adding to a stir fry – flavoured with oyster sauce.

Tufted on tree trunks and branches; cap greyish to deep violet; gills white, stemless

Spore print

Cap semicircular or shell-shaped, gradually becoming flattened with a wavy margin, whitish to greyish brown, blue-grey or even deep violet, smooth and dry

Gills decurrent, white, broad, and moderately crowded

No stem, or very short and laterally attached, thick and solid

5–14 cm

The Oyster Mushroom may be found throughout the year as it is resistant to low temperatures, but often occurs as abundant tiered shelves on fallen logs after the first rains of autumn. It grows in tight clusters on the trunks of broadleaved trees, and may appear in the same place over the years. The wide variation in colour can make identification confusing, but the shell-shaped cap and white gills should be distinctive. It is one of the few wild mushrooms to be successfully grown commercially, and it is possible to buy logs that have been innoculated with the mycelium to be grown into fruitbodies at home.

COOKING AND EATING The flesh has a mild mushroom flavour, and the texture and taste combine well with strong flavours, such as in this kedgeree. Slice 250 g Oyster Mushrooms and fry in butter with some crushed garlic. Cook 1 cup of rice in vegetable stock, with a pinch of saffron or turmeric and a bay leaf. Fry a chopped onion in butter with 1 teaspoon of curry powder or ground cumin, coriander and cayenne pepper. Drain the rice, add it to the onion, mix well and add 1 beaten egg, stirring gently until the egg is lightly cooked. Add half a cup of cream and the mushrooms and serve for breakfast.

Habitat: *On stumps and trunks of frondose trees, especially beech and poplar.*

LOOKALIKES

Blue Oyster Mushroom

Blue Oyster Mushroom
Pleurotus columbinus Very similar to the
oyster but with a bluish cap. Edible.

Green Oyster Mushroom
Panellus serotinus A winter species,
surviving early frosts. Cap olive green, slimy,
gills yellow, crowded. Inedible.

**Soft Slipper
Toadstool**
*Crepidotus
mollis* One of the
larger slipper
toadstools, on
dead branches,
with white gills becoming
cinnamon brown. Cap 2–7
cm in diameter, kidney
shaped, pale yellowish-
brown, with an elastic
pellicle; spore deposit snuff
brown. Inedible, though not
poisonous.

*Soft Slipper
Toadstool*

Velvet Shank

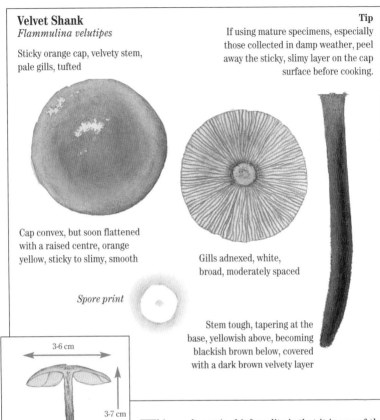

Velvet Shank
Flammulina velutipes

Sticky orange cap, velvety stem,
pale gills, tufted

Tip
If using mature specimens, especially
those collected in damp weather, peel
away the sticky, slimy layer on the cap
surface before cooking.

Cap convex, but soon flattened
with a raised centre, orange
yellow, sticky to slimy, smooth

Gills adnexed, white,
broad, moderately spaced

Spore print

Stem tough, tapering at the
base, yellowish above, becoming
blackish brown below, covered
with a dark brown velvety layer

3-6 cm

3-7 cm

0.3-0.5 cm

This mushroom's chief quality is that it is one of the very few that can be found in the depths of winter, even in January when there is little else for the wild food gatherer to harvest. It is resistant to frost, and can therefore be frozen at home, and revived in a reasonable condition upon thawing. It grows in tufts on tree stumps, especially those of Elm trees that have succumbed to Dutch Elm Disease and have been cut down. It has a rather insubstantial, slippery texture, but the flavour has been likened to white pepper and lemon. It is extremely popular in Japan, where it is cultivated under the name 'Enoki-taki'. These cultivated forms are almost pure white, etiolated with long, thin stems and tiny caps, and tufted together like a sort of shaving brush, looking nothing like the wild, fully grown variety. They are available in some supermarkets and oriental grocers.

COOKING AND EATING Try either the cultivated or the wild variety in a clear soup made from good chicken stock (including half a glass of dry sherry), and flavoured with star anise, galangal, chilli and lemon grass. Throw in the mushrooms a few minutes before serving, as they do not require much cooking. The soup may be served with noodles or, in a delicious mix of cultures, pasta parcels such as tortelloni.

Habitat: Tufted on deciduous trees, especially Elm.

LOOKALIKES

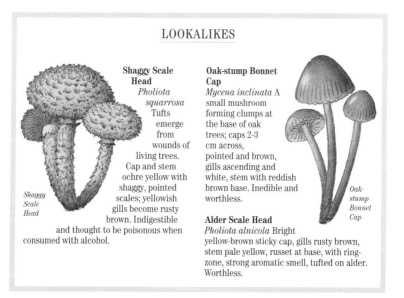

Shaggy Scale Head
Pholiota squarrosa Tufts emerge from wounds of living trees. Cap and stem ochre yellow with shaggy, pointed scales; yellowish gills become rusty brown. Indigestible and thought to be poisonous when consumed with alcohol.

Shaggy Scale Head

Oak-stump Bonnet Cap
Mycena inclinata A small mushroom forming clumps at the base of oak trees; caps 2-3 cm across, pointed and brown, gills ascending and white, stem with reddish brown base. Inedible and worthless.

Alder Scale Head
Pholiota alnicola Bright yellow-brown sticky cap, gills rusty brown, stem pale yellow, russet at base, with ring-zone, strong aromatic smell, tufted on alder. Worthless.

Oak-stump Bonnet Cap

Common Oyster

Common Oyster
Ostrea edulis

The two halves (called valves) of the Common Oyster are slightly different, one shallower and flatter than the other. They are variable in shape, though more or less circular, with a strongly sculpted surface, up to 10 cm across.

Portuguese Oyster
Crassostrea angulata

Now widely farmed, this species has a more elongated shape than the Common Oyster, with one valve acting like a flatter 'lid' over the other. Up to 15 cm long.

The inside of the shell has a shiny 'mother of pearl' finish.

Cooking
Oysters may be cooked on a wire rack over an open fire, and are ready when the shells open. Eat straight out of the shell with a dash of Tabasco sauce.

Up to 10 cm wide

Wild Oysters are a rare find these days on the lower shore of rocky places. At one time they were regarded as the food of the poor, being widely available for those with the time and energy to look for them. They then achieved luxury status as the social climate changed, but have now become reasonably priced again with the advent of farming them in special beds. It is mostly the Portuguese Oyster that is farmed, originally from the Bay of Biscay but now introduced to many places in Europe. The young Oysters are cemented on to ropes which are suspended in the water. When they have grown big enough, they are hauled up.

The Common Oyster is still farmed in a few places, and anywhere with suitable substrate close to such areas is the most likely place to find them. Like other bivalves such as the Mussel and Cockle, Oysters are filter feeders, so should be avoided when the seas are warm, especially as they are most likely to be seen in estuaries, which may be polluted.

COOKING AND EATING Oysters really are best treated simply: prise them open with a strong, blunt knife; gently scrape the flesh away from the shell, and swallow whole, with a squeeze of lemon if preferred.

The Common Oyster *occurs in shallow water in dense beds, on muddy, gravelly or stony situations such as estuaries, sometimes exposed during the lowest tides. The empty shells are frequently washed up on the beaches – a useful clue that there may be live ones further down the shore.*

Common Oyster

RANGE: The Mediterranean, Atlantic, English
Channel and North Sea.

COLLECTING PERIOD: October to April, or
whenever the sea water is cold.

Common Mussel

Common Mussel
Mytilus edulis

The shell size varies greatly, from 1 cm to 10 cm long, though this is not necessarily a guide to the size of the animal inside. The shells are attached by numerous threads – the beard. They often have barnacles attached to their outside surface.

Mussels grow in dense colonies, tightly packed together.

Usually blue-black, though often with brown patches. The inside of the shell is pearly, with a dark border.

Preparation
The beard needs to be trimmed before cooking, best done by gripping between the thumb and a blunt knife and giving it a sharp tug. Barnacles attached to the shell are harmless but unsightly. If you like good presentation, they should be scraped off if the mussels are to be served in their shells.

Up to 10 cm long

Mussels are slightly unusual among shellfish as they remain anchored to the same spot for most of their lives. They produce a bunch of tough threads from their foot, called the beard (the *byssus*), and this holds them fast to rocks or any immovable object, allowing them to open their valves and filter feed. Mussels are probably responsible for more cases of shellfish food-poisoning than anything else, as they concentrate toxins and bacteria in their guts, so should only be gathered from clean sea areas and only when the water is fairly cold.

Those growing in sandy places should be left in fresh water for an hour or two to allow them to clean themselves. They may contain tiny pearls, which are irritating for the diner so are best avoided if possible.

COOKING AND EATING For a classic *moules marinière*, sauté a little garlic in olive oil for a few minutes, add a glass of wine and one of water and bring to the boil. Add the Mussels, no more than two or three deep, so add in batches if necessary, and cover the pan. Check them after 3-5 minutes, when they should have opened, and remove with a slotted spoon, discarding any that fail to open. Add a dash of cream and fresh parsley to the liquor in the pan, and serve as a sauce, straining through muslin if sandy.

The Common Mussel is one of the easiest of shellfish to find, growing in dense colonies on stones, rocks, piers, jetties and breakwaters. They can be pulled or prised off with a knife, but avoid collecting from areas where there may be sewage outfalls or any kind of pollution, and ensure that the beach has been designated 'safe' by the local authorities.

Common Mussel

RANGE: The Mediterranean, Atlantic, English Channel, North Sea and Baltic.

COLLECTING PERIOD: October to April, or whenever the sea is cold (further details in the Introduction, page 14).

Common Cockle

Common Cockle
Cerastoderma edule

The two valves are joined together. They are distinctly heart-shaped and strongly curved.

The shell is up to 5 cm long, with longitudinal ridges that run from the apex to the margin. These correspond to short grooves on the inside of the shell.

Fawn or pale brown in colour, with slightly darker bands towards the margin. The inside of the shell is white with brown marks.

Gathering
Cockles live just below the surface so need to be brought up using a garden rake, or a rake fashioned from a piece of wood with 10 cm nails driven through it and a handle. Try several areas to discover one that is rich in Cockles, then rake backwards and forwards, carefully placing the exposed Cockles in a bucket (do not throw them).

Up to 5 cm long

The Cockle is a filter feeder like the Mussel (page 240). It lies buried just below the surface in sand or mud, projecting two siphons like periscopes up into the water, filtering plankton. It is difficult to determine exactly where Cockles will be found, but wide, flat areas of mud and sand close to tidal estuaries are the most likely places. Cockles often contain a lot of sand, so should be purged by keeping them in a bucket of sea water for several hours followed by a rinse in fresh water, discarding any that fail to close tight when disturbed.

COOKING AND EATING Cockles are not quite as tasty as Mussels, but worthwhile nevertheless. They can be cooked in the same way: by steaming or boiling in water or wine – discarding any that fail to open properly. Eat them as they are, or add to another dish such as this *paella*-style concoction.

Sauté some onion, garlic and chilli in butter until soft, then add 1 cup of long grain rice and cook for a few minutes. Add a glass of white wine and boil rapidly for two minutes, then add a cup of warm chicken stock and a can of chopped tomatoes. Simmer and stir until much of the liquid has been absorbed and the rice is cooked. Season well with salt and pepper and fresh parsley, adding the cooked Cockles at the end to warm them through.

The **Common Cockle** *lives buried in the damp sand or mud exposed at low tide, usually in estuaries or commercial beds, but only where the conditions are just right. The presence of empty shells further up the beach is a useful indicator, and sometimes live ones may be seen on the surface.*

Common Cockle

RANGE: The Mediterranean, Atlantic, English Channel and North Sea.

COLLECTING PERIOD: Best at the lowest, spring tides, and safest in the winter months.

Razor Shell

Razor Shell
Ensis siliqua

Gathering
Razor Shells are easiest caught when working with a partner, one handling the salt and the other grabbing the shell. You can then cook them fresh (after cleaning, see below) on a wire rack over a beach fire, with no more than lemon juice and black pepper as an accompaniment.

The colour of the external shell is off-white, with brown markings, but there is a greenish-brown layer called the periostracum which covers most of it. The inside of the shell is plain white.

The Curved Razor Shell (*Ensis ensis*) is smaller (up to 12 cm), and with a slight but distinct curve.

The shell is straight, up to 20 cm long, with both edges parallel to each other. There are fine grooves and ridges along the surface.

Up to 20 cm long

Razor Shells are a particularly delicious, meaty type of clam that is gaining in popularity with restaurants. However, they are relatively little known because they are so rarely seen alive. Although they live only a few centimetres below the surface of the sand at the extreme lower shore, they can use their strong muscular 'feet' to drag themselves down deep very rapidly, which they always do in response to the slightest vibration. They are too fast to dig up, but you can catch them using an excellent technique which requires little effort.

First, identify their burrows in the sand – marked by a hole with a shallow dimple around it, the size of a large coin. Using a dry funnel, pour a couple of tablespoons of table salt into the hole, and wash it down with a jet of water from a squeezable plastic bottle. The Razor Shell will shoot back up to the surface, protruding slightly, at which point it can be grabbed and put in a bucket. It may take a minute or two for the animal to respond, so several holes can be treated while waiting.

COOKING AND EATING The Razor Shells will need to be purged of sand by leaving them in clean sea water for a few hours, and then rinsing in fresh water. Cook them like Mussels. The entire animal can be eaten, though the large, meaty foot is the best part.

The **Razor Shell** occurs at the extreme lower end of the shore and below, so is usually only attainable during the lowest spring tides. They are never visible above the surface of the sand, but give away their presence by a shallow 2 cm dimple in the sand with a small hole in the centre.

Razor Shell

RANGE: The Mediterranean, Atlantic, English Channel and North Sea.

COLLECTING PERIOD: At any time, but best when the sea water is cold.

Common Limpet

Common Limpet
Patella vulgata

The single shell is cone-shaped, up to 7 cm high. It is pale grey or fawn in colour, with strong radiating ridges running from the apex to the margin.

Other species of limpet include those with a small hole in the shell's apex, or with tortoiseshell patterning or bright blue streaks on the shell, though, unlike the Common Limpet, they are not found on the upper shore.

Use
A satisfying way to eat Limpets is to put them directly in the embers of a beach fire and leave them there for half an hour or so, perhaps while preparing another dish. They can then be dragged out with a stick, the ash rubbed off, and eaten as they are with garlic and melted butter.

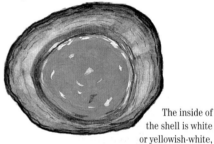

The inside of the shell is white or yellowish-white, with a brownish-silver scar left by the point at which the animal inside attaches itself.

Up to 7 cm high

Limpets are extremely common on any rocky coast, and very easy to find, so it is a pity that they don't taste especially good. They are inclined to be rather tough, but with suitable treatment can be made edible, and are certainly on the list of essential 'survival' food. It is difficult to remove them from the rock to which they are attached. Limpets graze on algae on the rock surface, moving about as the tide retreats, but returning to exactly the same spot, even rotating their shells into the same position, so that over time the shell wears a perfectly-fitting slot in the rock. On hard stone, the shell shapes itself to fit the surface contours of the rock.

Although the animal may 'peep' out of its shell when at rest, the slightest movement or vibration nearby makes it clamp down hard. Some say that it is possible to sneak up stealthily on limpets, and knock them off with a kind of karate-chop, using the side of the hand. This is the easiest way to severely injure your hand. Better to use a stout blade to prise them off.

COOKING AND EATING Limpets should be soaked in fresh water for a period, then put into rapidly boiling water and cooked until the meat comes free from the shell. It is then worth briefly frying them to tenderise the meat a little further.

Common Limpets *are abundant on rocky shores, always attached to the rocks themselves, from the upper tidal zone downwards. Specimens become progressively smaller and flatter further down the shore, perhaps because they have adapted to the increasing strength of the waves.*

Common Limpet

RANGE: The Atlantic, English Channel and
North Sea.

COLLECTING PERIOD: Safest collected from
October to April.

Index

Index

Other Books in the *Easy Nature Guides* series:

Easy Edible Mushroom Guide
Covering Britain and Europe
Features edible and poisonous species

Easy Tree Guide
Covering Britain and Europe
Features all the common species

Easy Wildflower Guide
Covering Britain and Europe
Features all the commonly found species

Easy Butterfly Guide
Covering Britain and Europe
Features all the commonly found species

Photography credits

Additional photography provided by:

Alamy Ltd
www.alamy.com
30 (Blickwinkel), 58 (Blickwinkel),
188 (Dynamic Graphics Group/IT Stock Free)

Biopix
www.biopix.dk
64, 100, 102, 104, 124, 126, 144, 176, 184, 190, 192, 198, 204, 208, 212

Fotolia
www.fotolia.co.uk
72 (Lidija Petrov)

Josef Hlasek: 234

Nature Picture Library
www.naturepl.com
130 (Bernard Castelein), 186 (Duncan McEwan), 202 (George McCarthy),
206 (Reinhard/ARCO), 216 (George McCarthy), 238 (Jose B. Ruiz), 240
(Julian Partridge), 242 (Christophe Courteau)

NHPA Ltd
www.nhpa.co.uk
54 (Laurie Campbell), 56 (Matt Bain), 62 (Brian Hawkes), 78 (Jordi Bas
Casas), 132 (Trevor McDonald), 134 (Laurie Campbell), 138 (Roy Waller),
140 (Mike Lane), 142 (Mark Bowler), 146 (Jim Bain), 210 (Darek Karp), 232
(Daniel Heuclin), 244 (Roy Waller), 246 (Gerry Cambridge)

Warren Photographic
www.warrenphotographic.co.uk
136 (Kim Taylor)